DISCOVERING SIX DAYS

A STORY ABOUT A MOTORCYCLE, FRIENDSHIP, AND ISDT HISTORY

KEITH GEISNER

Discovering Six Days

ISBN-13: 9781737948520 (pb)
ISBN-13: 9781737948506 (hc)

www.529bookdesign.com

ACKNOWLEDGMENTS

I'd like to thank Jim Simmons, Stan Rubottom, and their families and friends for helping me put the pieces together of their motorcycle racing past.

I'd also like to thank my beautiful wife, Sara, for joining me on yet another adventure into off-road motorcycle racing history.

DISCOVERING SIX DAYS

KEITH GEISNER

CONTENTS

PREFACE

You wake up in a foreign country forgetting where you are because, less than twenty-four hours ago, you were back in your own bed, in your own country, on your own sleep schedule, wrestling with anxiety about the days to come and wishing you could fall back asleep. Instead, your mind fills with thoughts of everything that's happened in the past year of competitive off-road racing: The hours of travel from qualifier to qualifier. The time away from family. The lost wages from skipping out of work to pursue your dreams. The ups and downs, injuries, and mechanical failures that have plagued you along the way.

Now, you made it to the big dance. All that hard work has paid off, but there's still work to be done. Your biggest challenge has yet to come. At this point, you are already a winner; you are one of the best off-road motorcycle riders in your country. But to finish this next challenge, you will have to dig deeper than ever before.

In the next six days, you will be all by yourself. Man against machine against Mother Nature. Only you have what it takes to finish. Only you can maintain your motorcycle's pace. It is up to you to be mentally fit and stay focused throughout the course of events. Only you can decide which path to take through the obstacles that await you.

This isn't just any event—it's what some call the Olympics of motorcycle racing. It's one of the most grueling off-road motorcycle races in history. You will be riding over 200 miles a day for six straight days in some of the worst terrains a motorcycle can navigate, all the while maintaining the endurance to push to the next checkpoint and the skill to perform all your own maintenance in an allowable amount of time. Did you pack the right tools? Did you pack extra spare parts? If it can break out there, it will.

You made it this far, no turning back.

Welcome to Six Days!

INTRODUCTION

Memories of my youth are similar, I imagine, to a lot of other kids who choose two-wheels to have fun on while growing up—they're epic.

If you grew up in the farming community of Ste. Genevieve, Missouri, and were into off-road motorcycle riding like I was, there's a good chance you heard about St. Joe State Park in Flat River. St. Joe Park was an off-road riding park that was always a topic of discussion. I would hear about my uncle racing there during the annual Flat River Grand Prix and how, when he took second place in his class one year, he did it crossing the finish line with a flat front tire. Or there are stories about one of his buddies who would cut trails to see how far ahead he could get

before being caught, over and over. Seeing my uncle and his friends' trophies on display added to my excitement, as did the photos that hung in my father's office of him climbing a mountain of chat in his dune buggy with the front tires almost vertical. I was too young to ever see these photos or stories in action, so, growing up, I lived to hear about this magical place to ride off-road.

My Uncle's pin from the first year of the Flat River Grand Prix held at St. Joe State Park. Photo by Keith Geisner

It felt like eons before I was old enough to actually experience St. Joe State Park. In reality, it was when I turned sixteen in 1993 and got my driver's license. Up to that point, I rode the surrounding farmlands of my neighbor's property. My older twin brothers, Jeff and John, and I had wide-open fields with terraces to jump, virgin woods to cut our own trails, and endless cow paths to follow. It was an awesome time in our lives and we had plenty of space to wet our riding appetites.

The day I finally got to ride at St. Joe State Park was like no other. Several of my high school buddies and I took off, tearing across the flats and up into the woods wearing nothing but blue jeans, t-shirts, and helmets. Back then you didn't feel pain when you were having that much fun. This was also the first time I got to ride a modern two-stroke, which was my friend's, and it gave me a thrill you can't put into words. That first visit to St. Joe Park started a weekend ritual for us. Also, now that I got a taste of the two-stroke powerband, I was itching to ride different bikes, as well. The type of riding I did while growing up turned out to be good training for my racing ambitions that were to come.

My Dad having fun in his dune buggy at St. Joe State Park. Photo by Keith Geisner

After college, I was in the market for a new bike. I had experience riding both two-strokes and four-strokes, so I knew what I liked and didn't like in a bike. At the time, the new Yamaha WR400F was released and getting great reviews. My buddy Tim Luttrell worked at the Yamaha dealership Surdyke Motorsports in Festus, Missouri. They had a 1998 WR400F for sale that someone had just traded in, and Tim told me about it. I purchased the bike and fell in love. It had the exciting power of a two-stroke and the never-ending top-end and low-end grunt of a four-stroke. It was the best of both worlds.

Around this time, I was working at Chrysler, and some co-workers who rode off-road were talking about the upcoming hare scramble race right in Festus. I had wanted to race a hare scramble since listening to my uncle's stories as a kid. This hare scramble was hosted by Surdyke Motorsports. I showed up unprepared, entered the beginner's class, and away I went. Throughout the entire race, I was loving it and couldn't wait to tell my brothers. After nine laps without stopping for a drink, I pulled off before attempting the last lap and downed a bottle of water. Then, about halfway through the last lap, my body started shutting down. I pulled off to the side and let the beast of a motorcycle sit there, cool down, and idle. The WR was ready and waiting for me to come to my senses. I finished that last lap, but it about killed me. It took everything I had to go collect my tenth-place cash award. As I lay behind my truck on the ground, my uncle's childhood friends, Wayne Kertz and Tim Arnold (who'd also raced hare scrambles in the past), came by and helped load my bike. I couldn't thank them enough. Even though I about died finishing that race, I learned a few things. I needed a softer seat—monkey butt is no joke—and I needed a CamelBak to stay hydrated throughout the race. The next day, I couldn't stop thinking about how exciting that race was. I was hooked. The thrill of competing and challenging oneself on a motorcycle is an addicting feeling. For the next twenty years, my WR400F and I would partake in numerous hare scrambles and enduros across Missouri, but none would be hosted by the Surdyke family, as my first race was their last.

While racing in modern hare scrambles, I was introduced to vintage motocross. I was fortunate that Missouri also had a vintage motocross series already in place, run by Curtis Harper. I participated in my first vintage motocross in 2001. My first vintage bike—I was bit by the vintage bug—was a 1973 Honda CR250 Elsinore.

My first real encounter with vintage motorcycles started in the late 1990s when a friend of mine invited me over to go riding through the fields of his family's farm. I was new and learning everything I could about them. I showed up with my 1991 Kawasaki KX250, which really caught my friend's attention, and he really admired it. He took me over and opened the door to a massive barn to show me his bikes, and there were two Hondas with the name Elsinore on the sides of them. I was somewhat familiar with the make but didn't really know the significance of it. One had a silver tank with a green stripe, and the other had a silver tank with an orange stripe. The orange striped one also had a headlight and taillight. I knew right then this was the dawn of a long journey into riding and collecting vintage bikes.

The 1973 Honda CR250 that started it all. Photo by Keith Geisner

We tore off through the fields and woods that day. We had an awesome time, as there seemed to be an endless amount of land to explore. It reminded me of the beach scene in the movie *On Any Sunday*. At the end of the day, my friend asked if he could take my KX for a spin, and I said sure. He headed out on the bike and fell in love with it. Since I had an internal draw toward the Elsinores, and he liked my KX, we decided to trade. I loaded up his two Elsinores and my KX found a new home in his barn.

Since that day, countless motorcycles have been loaded into the back of my truck that have either been restored, traded, or sold to fund my next motorcycle project.

Two of these motorcycles have come with so much off-road racing history tied to them, I'm compelled to bring their stories to light.

These bikes weren't your run-of-the-mill motorcycles, and both were so unique with one thing in common: America. One was raced by an American motocross team, and the other was raced while representing America in the International Six Day Trial (ISDT). The motocross bike took me on an incredible journey, which I wrote about in my first book, *Finding #49 and America's Forgotten Motocross Team*. This motorcycle ended up being a Harley-Davidson motocross team bike and the journey I took preserving the history of that bike was quite the experience. Serial numbers don't lie and, if you read my first book, you know that a serial number can make all the difference in a bike's history. But what do you do when your newly acquired, vintage motorcycle doesn't have a serial number? How do you trace its path? Well, luckily for me, I didn't need one.

Discovering Six Days is a story about a motorcycle that led to the discovery of new friends with stories and friendships to last a lifetime. This motorcycle opened the door to the world of racing history with which I was not familiar, and it took me full circle back to where it all began, St. Joe State Park.

Now in my forties, I still crave the competitiveness of off-road motorcycle racing. The respect I have for others who have raced before me and for the untold history of the sport is what has compelled me to tell this story.

Harley-Davidson MX team bike #49. Photo by Keith Geisner

ISDT

Back in the 1970s, there were thousands of off-road motorcycle riders around the United States who competed throughout the year to have the chance to qualify to race in the International Six Day Trial, more commonly known as the ISDT. Some missed the opportunity by seconds due to bad luck, mechanical failures, injury, and the ever-increasing competition. Before even making it to the ISDT, one must endure a series of two-day qualifiers in the U.S. Two-Day Trial Championship Series, which is held throughout the United States. One day, a rider could be racing a qualifier in Oregon and, a few weeks later, they could be competing in New Jersey. At the end of the qualifying rounds, only the top thirty to forty riders out of 4,000 or more got to represent the USA in the ISDT. The time and commitment sacrificed by these riders is unprecedented, given less than 1 percent make it to the actual ISDT race.

I'm fortunate to live in an area in the Midwest—and Missouri, specifically—that has historically been a hot bed for bigtime ISDT riders, with last names such as Mungenast, Surdyke, Schmidt, Simmons, Rubottom, Hagerty, Fogle, and Clark to name a few. If you would have asked me who these riders were before Fall 2017, I probably wouldn't have been able to name half of them, but, because of a lucky discovery in October 2017, the world of ISDT cracked wide open for me.

• • •

They call it the Olympics of motorcycling. The ISDT is the oldest motorcycling competition in the history of the sport. In 1897, the Automobile Club of Great Britain and Ireland was founded, and they organized an "Emancipation Run" of vehicles to Brighton. By 1900, in three short years, the event developed to become the "Great 1,000 Miles Trial" for two-, three-, and four-wheeled machines. By 1903, this "club," which was ninety-three members strong, set up the Auto Cycle Union (ACU) to become the governing body of motorcycle sport. The ACU Six Days Reliability Trial took place that year and became an annual event. In 1913, with further growth, the event was placed under the jurisdiction of the Fédération Internationale de Motocyclisme (FIM), which had been founded in 1904 in Paris (later moving to Switzerland). They renamed it the International Touring Trial, the ancestor of what was to become the ISDT (the initial format would remain for many years). This inaugural event in 1913 was held in Carlisle, England.

NATIONAL TEAM COLORS

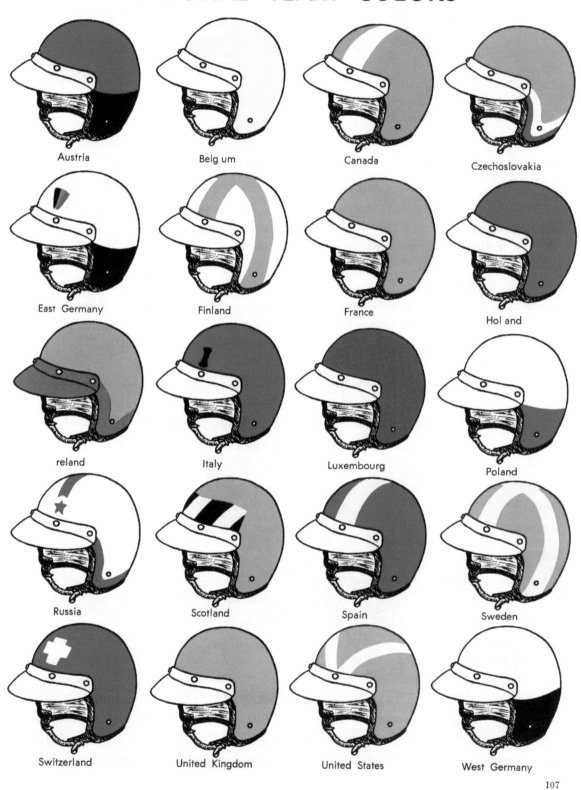

Austria

Belg um

Canada

Czechoslovakia

East Germany

Finland

France

Hol and

reland

Italy

Luxembourg

Poland

Russia

Scotland

Spain

Sweden

Switzerland

United Kingdom

United States

West Germany

107

ISDT National Team Helmet colors. Photo by the American Motorcyclist Association

In 1980, the name changed to International Six Day Enduro (ISDE) to reflect developments in the sport.[1]

Although originally an on-road competition, the earliest events would have taken place on Pre-WW1 country lanes with motorcycles that were lacking in the suspension, power, and braking departments—areas we take for granted today with the advancements in motorcycle technology.

The exact rules have changed over the years but, in its original conception, riders competed in country teams, requiring them to use motorcycles from their specific country—i.e., Germany on German machines (BMW) and Spain on Spanish machines (Ossa, Bultaco). As the number of manufacturers dwindled, these rules were relaxed, and now any country can use machines of their choice.

The competition is still held over six days, with over 1,250 miles typically covered over the duration of the event. Riders must compete over a fixed route while travelling between two points within a fixed time period. In addition to the long days of riding, contestants are subjected to acceleration, racing, and hill climbing tests, where they are measured for all-out speed, for which they earn "evaluation points." When competing, there are strict rules on outside assistance, requiring the rider to service their own motorcycle, having tools and spare parts on them. During the event, a rider is not allowed to make any significant repairs to their motorcycle. Major components on each machine are marked to prevent tampering, other than replacing tires, tubes, cables, and drive chains. Each motorcycle competing in the ISDT has to go through tech inspection. To avoid parts from being swapped out throughout the course of the event, all parts of each motorcycle get marked with paint dabs and the rider's number is scribed into the bike's fresh paint dabs. This makes it easy to tell if a rider is cheating. Also, the motor's head is sealed onto the cylinder with a wire and lead seal. If the wire is missing or cut, the judges know the rider has swapped out a piston or top end.

One has to pray their motorcycle will last the full six days. For this reason, riders have to understand how to avoid punishing their motorcycle under punishing conditions. Like an enduro, there are checkpoints throughout the course. If a rider arrives a single minute late, he loses a "mark." To earn a gold medal, one must complete the event with a perfect score, having lost not a single minute from the prescribed schedule (over the course of nearly a thousand miles of extremely difficult riding). A rider can earn a silver medal by losing no more than twenty-five marks, plus evaluation points within the percentage range of his class. And, for just finishing the event within the hour of their "key time," a rider will earn a bronze medal. Just finishing is a victory in itself.[2]

Awards are given in the form of medals—gold, silver, bronze—to individuals, with country and manufacturer teams competing for trophies where there are various ones given depending on gender and team size, etc.

Europe was the exclusive domain of the event until 1973, when it made its way to the United States. The event has since been held outside the Old Country numerous times, including Chile, New Zealand, Brazil, the United States, and Australia.

Until the early 1960s, most American motorcyclists had not even heard of the ISDT, and few had ridden it. From 1920 through 1945, the American motorcycle industry, supported by the policies of the American Motorcyclist Association (AMA), simply regarded Six Days as an irrelevant, foreign activity that had nothing to do with motorcycling on this side of the Atlantic. This started to change when a handful of our nation's best off-road riders began to take an interest in the event. One of the first was New York BSA rider Tom McDermott, who entered the ISDT in Wales in 1949 and became the first American to win a gold medal.

However, such accomplishments remained obscure until *Cycle World* began to report on the involvement of Americans in international competition. In part, because he was accessible to the California-based media, Bud Ekins became the Marco Polo of off-road motorcycling. He had ridden scrambles in England and motocross in France in the early 1950s and entered the ISDT in Wales in 1961 with two other Americans, Jim Brunson and Lloyd Lingelbach. Bud Ekins and Jim Brunson won silver medals. This wasn't easy, because the AMA had no affiliation with the International Motorcycling Federation, so American riders had to jump through difficult administrative and diplomatic hoops to participate. For example, to ride in the 1962 ISDT, John Penton had to obtain his international license through Canada. The 1964 American team of Bud Ekins, Dave Ekins, Cliff Coleman, Steve McQueen followed by Bruce Brown's movie, *On Any Sunday*, and the Penton family were all key players in the off-road revolution that swept American motorcycling.[3]

Throughout the 1960s, there were no qualifying rounds for Americans to attend to receive the honor of competing in the ISDT. These U.S. riders had to be hand-selected and/or supported by private individuals, companies, or motorcycle manufacturers. That all changed in 1971, when the AMA created a national series of events where riders had to earn points to qualify for the Six Day. If qualifying scores were close, the AMA became the tie breaker, and the FIM set rider quotas for the various nations. The United States was limited to around thirty-five riders. And, by mid-1970s, more than 600 riders were attending each qualifier to earn their place on the American team. Now it required a serious commitment of time and resources to ride qualifying rounds throughout the Unites States and earn a place within the American contingent.

A series of two-day qualifiers was started to find the best of the best in the United States to represent America in the ISDT. Starting in 1971, the first official two-day qualifier was at Trask Mountain in McMinnville, Oregon. There was only one two-day qualifier in 1971, but more qualifiers were added to the schedule by 1972. Throughout the 1970s, riders would compete from coast to coast in locations such as an Army base in Fort Hood, Texas; Bad Rock in Weston, Oregon; Shamrock in Barstow, California; Trask Mountain in McMinnville, Oregon; Rose City, Michigan; "Broken Piston" in Potosi, Missouri; and Picayune, Mississippi. This new form of off-road racing exposed more Americans to the national scene. Names that were never heard of were now popping up in motorcycle magazines across America. Talented riders were being discovered by motorcycle manufactures and given the opportunity to compete on the world stage of racing while being sponsored and supported.

It was these two-day qualifiers that ultimately paved the way for up and coming off-road riders to the national stage—and what ultimately led to a dynamic duo from Esther, Missouri.

(Right) Jim Simmons at the Austria 1976 ISDT. Photo by Patrick Tran-Duc

Finding Jim Simmons

Like many great stories, mine started with a series of seemingly inconsequential events that ultimately came together in the end.

I had been looking for my next project—my Harley-Davidson factory MX bike was progressing nicely—when I came across a 1978 Yamaha YZ400 listed on Facebook Marketplace by a guy named Johnny Waller. Johnny had the YZ priced right, but my time to go and fetch motorcycles was limited due to having two small children—my son Rex, two, and my daughter Eden, seven months. So, I sent Johnny a note to see if he would deliver it if I doubled his asking price—yes, it was priced that good in my opinion. He said yes. A time and date were set for the delivery.

The day came when Johnny was to deliver the motorcycle. As he pulled in, I was surprised to see an older gentleman with a big white beard driving the truck. It was Johnny, but he just didn't fit the image I had for someone with this vintage motocross bike. Come to find out—he had a deep history with off-road racing. Johnny Waller was from Potosi, Missouri. He told me that he and his close friend Tom Clark used to ride motorcycles, and that Tom eventually taught him blacksmithing. I wasn't aware of who Tom Clark was at the time. The more we talked, Johnny became comfortable with telling me about a few other bikes he was considering selling. One of them was Jim Simmons' 1976 ISDT WR360 Husqvarna, which still had the inspection paint marks on it. I knew a little about the ISDT, but I wasn't familiar with the name Jim Simmons. Johnny said Jim lived in Farmington, Missouri, only thirty miles from me. It bothered me a little that I lived so close to a guy with motorcycle history and never heard about him. At the time of this transaction, I was finishing up a preservation restoration of a Harley-Davidson MX team bike I'd found a year earlier, so to possibly run across another motorcycle of historical significance was unheard of. I told Johnny my story about the Harley-Davidson MX team bike and showed him the current stage the preservation was in. Johnny was particularly interested in my story and felt that his Jim Simmons bike should be treated with the same care and detail. We bonded over our interest in motorcycles and, by the time he left, he had plans to send me pictures of his other bikes.

The next morning, I got a text message from Johnny with pictures of three bikes and some extra parts. He gave me a price for each item individually and a price if I'd buy the whole lot. He said he'd give me a day to decide before he puts everything on Facebook Marketplace. A few of those photos were of the Jim Simmons bike, and you could see the inspection paint marks Johnny had made note of. I asked where he got the Simmons bike. He said that he purchased it from a co-worker named Tom Reeves, who went by the nickname "Craz." I knew Tom Reeves through my years of buying and selling vintage motorcycles. He and his friend Dennis Degonia would always come to the motorcycle swap meets I hosted. Johnny said Tom had just passed away two weeks prior, so it was sad news to learn. Tom was always a joy to talk bikes with. I'm not sure how Tom got the Simmons bike, but I know that he and Dennis bought, sold, and collected motorcycles, so it made sense. The clock was ticking, and I needed to get some information on this Simmons Husqvarna to verify it was the real deal. The first thing that popped in my head was that I needed to determine who this Jim Simmons guy is and find out if he raced this Husqvarna at the 1976 ISDT in Zeltweg, Austria. I started Googling Jim Simmons. I got a lot of hits, but most of them showed him racing a Rokon motorcycle in the ISDT. Rokon was a motorcycle I didn't hear a lot about.

First photo received with inspection markings on the Jim Simmons bike. Photo by Johnny Waller

• • •

As with any purchase, I needed to do my homework. Rokon was certainly a bike I'd heard of, but I wanted to know more about the company's history. When one hears the name Rokon, the first thing that comes to mind are those two-wheel drive motorcycles called Trail-Breakers you see in the back of hunting magazines, but there was a short time in Rokon's history when they were producing motorcycles strictly for competitive racing.

From the website *rokonworld.com*, I learned the history of Rokon started with the Trailmaker two-wheel-drive motorcycle. It can be traced back to around 1958 when Charles Fehn of San Bernardino, California, began work on his invention.

Nethercutt Industries purchased Charles Fehn's designs and rebranded it Trail-Breaker. The very first Trail-Breaker built by Rokon was produced in February 1966 with the serial number MK302001. Rokon was on its way! In 1969, Rokon mailed out their first newsletter, *TRACKS*. The newsletter would be printed sporadically with a total of eighteen issues, the last dated October 1975. The newsletters featured Trail-Breakers, their owners and experiences, maintenance tips by Shop Foreman Reggie Bishop, and introduced Rokon's new models and accessories.

In 1970, Nick Harris obtained majority control of the company and in May of 1971 embarked on a project to develop a motorcycle for that portion of the motorcycle market not dominated by the Japanese, a competitive "enduro" bike. The RT-340 was quickly developed and successfully racing by September 1971 when it won the AMA-sanctioned enduro event at Talladega, Alabama. The RT-340 was first in class, second overall and the trophy was said to be taller than the rider, Tom Clark.

Could this be the same Tom Clark that Johnny Waller grew up next to? More on Tom later.

The RT-340 required a fresh build sheet. The drive train was chosen first and the chassis second. The engine was a Sachs model used to power snowmobiles, a 334cc two-stroke single. It was a four-port engine—intake, two transfer, exhaust—along with two booster ports which helped send the mixture toward the exhaust, creating a better burn. Built tough, it had the crankshaft running on ball bearings. In 1973, Rokon used an American Tillotson 38mm carburetor, but soon found a 36mm Mikuni worked better. Compression ratio was said to be 11.2:1, using the European full-stroke measuring system, whereas the Japanese exhaust-port measurement would read about 7.2:1—quite a difference in numbers, not compression.

Starting this engine was a new experience for riders, as it used a pull rope—like on a snowmobile or lawnmower. Various starting techniques were developed, one of the more popular being to stand on the left side of the bike, left hand reaching across to the right end of the handlebar, keeping the throttle closed and the front brake on, right hand grabbing the T-handle on the end of the rope. Pull! It might take a few pulls when cold, usually one pull when warm. Once running, if the rider wanted to "cleanse" the engine with a bit of a rev, he could lean the bike onto the kickstand, lift the rear wheel off the ground, and rev away.

Throw a leg over the saddle, twist the throttle, and the torque converter was intended to start functioning at about 2,800 rpm. The more spin, the more centrifugal force, the harder the bite, with the engine designed to turn happily at a competitive 6,000-6,700 rpm all day long, maximizing the torque automatically. Rokon said the engine put out 37 horses at the crankshaft, figuring about 30 at the rear wheel. A normal dyno test was not possible, as a compensator in the "tranny" always adjusted for rear-wheel load. Conversely, when the throttle was backed off, the RT was in free-wheeling mode…no compression braking. A #530 chain was used to connect the counter sprocket to the rear wheel.

The chassis was quite conventional, the drivetrain sitting in a cradle frame made of steel tubing, with a wheelbase of 57 inches. The Spanish company Betor supplied the fork and twin shocks, the fork being raked at 30 degrees with trail of 4.7 inches, the shocks having three-way preload. Tires were a 3.25 x 19 knobby at the front, 3.50 x 18 at the back. And hydraulic disc brakes at both ends used single-action calipers and 11-inch discs; brakes were important because of the lack of engine braking.

A nice padded seat was added for the solo rider; no passenger pegs offered. On top of the triple clamp was space for three instruments, with a speedo/odometer, watch holder and an enduro route-chart holder. This was certainly intended as a competitor for the International

Six Days Trial, which just happened to be held in New England's Berkshire Hills in 1973. The RT did itself proud, with four medals. The RT-340 sold to the public for $1,645.

In an internal Rokon document titled "RT-340 Preliminary Market Analysis" from September 1971, Rokon saw a "one-billion-dollar market" they intended to tap and noted "the Rokon motorcycle (i.e., the RT-340) must sell at a high enough price to assure a 40 percent gross margin; it must be price competitive; it must perform equal to or better than its own particular competition, and it must be capable of inspiring end users to request dealers to stock it."

These were pretty lofty goals for a company that had no experience with traditional motorcycle production or sales.

By late 1971, and no-doubt spurred by a $260K net loss for the year mainly attributable to RT-340 development costs, Nick Harris had lost interest in the company and controlling interest in Rokon was obtained by E.R. Hampson. Bob Grip was company president, rider Tom Clark was on as vice president, and Orla Larsson was Rokon Director. The short-term business objective became for Rokon to live within its own cash flow and return to a profitable operation. By the end of the first quarter of 1972, and with the help of 416 Trail-Breaker sales during the period, the Trail-Breaker was showing a profit, but a loss was incurred by the continuing RT-340 development and racing program. Targeted at the very top end of the Enduro price range, the RT-340 program would bring Rokon to its knees.

Rokon would build a series of bikes based on the RT-340 which included the RT-340 TCR (Tom Clark Replica, the height of vanity), RT-340-I, RT-340-II, RX/C-340, street legal ST-340, motocross MX 340, MX-II GP, MX Cobra, and the FT 340 flat tracker.[4]

Rokon competed in ISDT qualifiers in 1971 and 1972 with Tom Clark being their lead rider developing the bike. In 1973, Rokon decided to assemble a team to take on the ISDT and Tom Clark was one of the guys deciding who would be on the team. First-year team members consisted of Jim Simmons, Jim Fogle, Stan Rubottom, and Gary Snider. More on the Rokon team to come.

• • •

As part of my research into Rokon, I found that Jim Simmons' name was very closely connected with the brand. It looked like he qualified and competed in the ISDT on a Rokon in 1973 and 1975. I finally ran across an article that said Jim qualified on a Rokon in 1976, but Rokon closed its doors and Jim lost his funding and his ride to the Austria ISDT. Jim ended up receiving a Husqvarna ride from Ed Schmidt. Who is Ed Schmidt, and could this be the same Husqvarna that Johnny had? After finding this news, I knew I was getting close, but I still needed hard evidence that this was the bike.

I reached out to my friend, Ray Mungenast, and sent him the only photos I had of the bike. Ray is not only an ISDE veteran but his father, Dave Mungenast, was also a decorated ISDT veteran. Ray responded that based on the number of different colored inspection marks on the bike, he believed it was a qualifier bike but not an actual ISDT bike. More on Ray's observation later.

I jumped on Facebook and started researching ISDT and Jim's name. I came across a group called Leroy Winters Memorial ISDT Reunion Ride. Who was Leroy Winters?

Leroy Winters was the first rider to win the Jack Pine Enduro aboard a lightweight motorcycle. He did it on a German-designed-but-Harley-Davidson-branded DKW 165. Winters was one of the first riders to capitalize on the bikes. He modified the motorcycle for the grueling Jack Pine Enduro and claimed victory in 1956. That was just the start of Winters' off-road success. Later in his racing career, the Fort Smith, Arkansas, rider became an international ambassador for U.S. off-road competition. He increased his prominence in the sport significantly by competing in the ISDT from the mid-1960s through 1972. He won a silver medal twice in the World Championship event riding for Team USA. Winters' connection to the ISDT was so enduring that in 1995 his club, the Razorback Riders in Arkansas, organized an ISDT reunion ride. Winters died in 1998, and the event was renamed the Leroy Winters Memorial.[5]

The April 1955 issue of *American Motorcyclist* had this to say about Winters: Little 135 lb. Leroy Winters of Fort Smith, Arkansas, lived up to the name of 'Arkansas Traveler' as he traveled over the rugged 70-mile Enduro course to win the Handlebar Derby event on a swinger-arm 165 Harley-Davidson to outclass a record field of more than 80 riders with a score of 971. Leroy Winters was inducted into the AMA Motorcycle Hall of Fame in 1999.[6]

The Leroy Winters' Memorial ISDT Reunion Ride group was the only group on Facebook I could find at the time that dealt with the ISDT. I requested to join and, within an hour, I was accepted. My first post asked if anyone knew Jim Simmons and, if so, how to get ahold of him. (I did not yet mention the Husqvarna.) Within minutes I got a private message from group member Jeff DeBell. Jeff's message gave me hope: "Hi Keith, Jim's daughter, April, is on Facebook but Jim is not. He lives in Farmington, Missouri. Jim is a great guy and tell him I said hello!" I went on to tell Jeff I believed I'd found one of Jim's bikes and sent him a picture of the Husqvarna. Jeff confirmed the multiple inspection paint marks and added he had a Jeff Hammond 1973 Can-Am ISDT bike, which was now at the Mungenast Automobile and Motorcycle Museum in St. Louis. I was very familiar with the Mungenast Museum. Now that I had Jim's daughter's name, it was time to track her down.

I found April on Facebook and sent her a message to tell her I found what could be one of her father's old race bikes and wanted to confirm the bike's history before I purchased it. The message read: "April, I came across a motorcycle your dad, Jim, may have raced in 1976 and would like to talk to you or your dad to get more information. Thanks, Keith." I also sent her the pictures I had gotten from Johnny Waller.

April responded: "Here is his number. He is at the lake fishing, so he probably doesn't have his phone handy and he is also hard of hearing, LOL. I remember a bike that looked just like that in our basement that he worked on. Brings back a lot of memories. He has quite the stories too! Spent many hours at races when I was a kid."

With the phone number April just gave me, I found a quiet place to talk and made the call. After a few rings, a lady answered. I asked her if Jim was available, and she said, "Yes, hold

Jim visiting the Rokon factory in Rochester, New Hampshire. Photo by Rokon International, Inc.

Jim Simmons riding for Rokon at a two-day qualifier.
Photo by Jim Simmons

on, we're in a boat fishing, let me hand the phone over." Jim answered and his voice was very deep and moving. Similar to Morgan Freeman's, but with a drawl. I introduced myself and explained to him about the Husqvarna motorcycle I had the opportunity to purchase. I told him who I was buying it from and who had it before him. Jim asked me what color the gas tank was and I told him purple. Right away, he said, "That was the bike I rode in the 1976 Austria ISDT." This was great news. Jim went on to say that the bike would not have a title or frame serial number. I found this story all so interesting. Jim told me he lived in Farmington. I asked if, after I got the bike, it would be okay to come down and interview him about his riding history. Jim said, "No problem, we'll be in Arkansas for a few more weeks and then home." Now that I confirmed the Jim Simmons bike, it was time to make the deal.

• • •

With the new information from Jim Simmons, I gave Johnny Waller a call and told him I'd do the package deal. He was happy to hear Jim was still around. We both had the following Friday available, so we agreed on that day for the pickup. Leading up to that, I kept researching Jim Simmons. I was amazed at the number of qualifiers and ISDT races he participated in throughout the 1970s (1973–1978). He received a bronze medal at the 48th ISDT, which took place in Dalton, Massachusetts, onboard a Rokon. In 1975, Jim qualified for the 50th ISDT with the Rokon team. It was at the Isle of Man, but Jim did not finish due to a badly damaged rim. In 1976, as stated previously, I found an article that explained how Jim qualified that year on his Rokon, but since Rokon shut down their business, his friend Ed Schmidt came through and supplied him with a Husqvarna, which Jim raced to a silver medal in the 51st ISDT in Austria. Jim's race number at the 1976 ISDT was 319. My research sort of faded after the 1976 season because I was mostly focused on Jim's Husqvarna motorcycle. But I did run across an article that showed Jim raced in the 53rd ISDT in Sweden aboard a Yamaha in 1978. More on Jim's ISDT history later.

Friday finally arrived, and I asked my dad if he'd like to ride along. Directions and arrival time were discussed with Johnny Waller, and we were on our way. It was a nice, cool autumn day in Missouri and, when we arrived at Johnny's place, there was still dew on the grass. Johnny was already out in his garage getting things organized. He had three bikes and a few boxes of items for me. Besides Jim Simmons' Husqvarna, Johnny had a 1969 Yamaha DT-1 that he got from his friend Tom Clark. He went on to tell me how he first met Tom and how he attended all the enduro races in the Potosi area back in the day. So, now I was putting the pieces together. The Tom Clark that Johnny was friends with was the same Tom Clark who'd worked at Rokon.

Johnny ended up with a few of Tom's things after he passed away, which included one of his ISDT helmets and a box of miscellaneous ISDT and AMA memorabilia. Johnny's collection of photos he had taken throughout the years was also in the box. The newest photos were taken at the 2006 ISDT reunion ride in Flat River, Missouri. The second bike was a 1974 Yamaha DT360 he'd bought several years ago from a person in town. It was all stock, complete, and had a title. And the third bike was Jim Simmons' 1976 Husqvarna. Jim was correct. There was no serial number on the frame. Why would there be no frame number

Tom Clark has announced his resignation from the position of Director of Professional Racing of the American Motorcycle Association. He served as department head of the Professional Racing Department since September, 1968.

Clark has resigned his staff position with the AMA to serve as Vice President in charge of sales at Rokon, Inc.

Tom Clark making his transition from the AMA to Rokon. Photo by the American Motorcyclist Association

on this bike? Not only did Johnny have Jim's bike, but he also had Jim's toolbox and a box of parts that went with the bike. It was a nice collection of items, and I was looking forward to going through everything and learning their place in history. We got it all loaded up and I told Johnny I'd keep him posted on my progress with Jim's bike. But, first, I had to finish the Harley-Davidson MX team bike I was in the middle of preserving.

• • •

I had to learn more about who this Tom Clark guy was if I was in possession of some of his racing items. The name sounded familiar, but I couldn't quite place him. Then it occurred to me that the previous owner of Jim's bike before Johnny Waller was Tom Reeves. I actually knew Tom and his good friend Dennis Degonia, as mentioned earlier. Tom and Dennis had purchased a few bikes from me in the past, too, and I would run into them at motorcycle events now and again. It's been a few years since I've seen them but, back in the early 2000s, I had a Can Am 175 TNT that I'd found and was debating whether to sell or fix up. Tom and Dennis had been at my house purchasing some Yamaha enduro parts when they spied the Can-Am. They both mentioned Tom Clark's name and said he would be interested in the bike. They said something about Tom's ISDT history. At the time, I had no idea what all the ISDT talk

Jim Simmons' Husqvarna placed on the stand with tank removed. Photo by Keith Geisner

encompassed. I gave Tom and Dennis my phone number to give to Clark. A few weeks went by before I received a call from Tom Clark, and we made arrangements to meet up. The day came when Tom Clark arrived to buy my Can-Am. I was surprised by his appearance. He wasn't very tall and, personally, I felt he looked a little too old to be even considering riding a motorcycle. Tom told me that he used to race a similar bike and that he wanted to fix this bike up to ride in the ISDT reunion ride at St. Joe Park, which was coming up soon. I didn't think much of it, sold him the Can-Am, and helped him load it up. Little did I know our paths would cross again over a decade later.

Johnny Waller first met Tom when he was trail riding his Yamaha LT1 100. They crossed paths on the trail when Tom was out practicing for an upcoming enduro. A friendship started, and many memories were made. Tom was a very busy person. Not only did he attend the 1971 ISDT at the Isle of Man to help guide Americans during their first entry as a country into the competition, but he also participated in the ISDT in 1972 at Czechoslovakia and 1973 when it was hosted by the USA. During that same time, he was the VP of sales and a development rider for Rokon. Before Tom's ISDT and Rokon riding days, you could find him racing on his BSA in the 1950s with the likes of Dick Mann—also one of the first riders to compete in the AMA Grand National Championship racing for Yamaha back in 1963. In between and after his competitive racing, Tom worked for the AMA based in Ohio. Some of the titles he held at the AMA were Director of Professional Racing and Marketing Manager. Tom had a weekend home in Potosi, where he rode and practiced blacksmithing. Johnny said that Tom would drive home on the weekends to ride and split wood. He would then haul the wood up to the AMA in Ohio and sell it. Johnny also showed me some blacksmithing tools that Tom had trained him on. He chose Missouri because of the riding environment and opportunities it presented.

Knowing what I knew now, I wish I would have spent more time with Tom. I would have loved to work on the Can-Am with him and learn from his past. Unfortunately, Tom passed away back in 2008 at the age of seventy-six.

• • •

Once I got home, my dad helped me get everything unloaded, and we said our goodbyes. Then, I placed Jim's Husqvarna on my bike lift, so I could get a better look at it and set up a table to go through all the boxes I got from Johnny. From years of going through boxes of parts, I've learned to "not throw anything away" because, later, you may kick yourself after realizing what you threw away had a significant history or was essential to what you were working on. In addition to the two boxes that came with Jim's bike, there was an extra exhaust pipe that I hung next to a shelf that I planned to put the rest of Jim's parts on. I pulled out Jim's toolbox and opened it up. It was like a time capsule that hadn't been opened in four decades. There were some homemade tools, some used and new parts. I just kind of took a mental

Box of extra parts received with Jim's bike. Photo by Keith Geisner

Jim's racing toolbox. Photo by Keith Geisner

Inside Jim's racing toolbox. Photo by Keith Geisner

inventory of what was there and then cleaned a place off on the shelf to store it. The next box I opened went with Jim's Husqvarna. It was a cardboard box full of extra parts: brake shoes, a rod kit still in the Husqvarna Styrofoam box, used pistons, air filter cages, and a number of other items. I was sort of confused because I couldn't understand what all the extra parts were for if he had just raced the bike in Austria at one Six Days race. I knew they couldn't swap rods during a Six Days. More research later will answer these questions.

The last two boxes were items Johnny received from Tom Clark. In these boxes, I found off-road riding magazines that Johnny had collected over the years, and photos he had taken at the Potosi enduro and ISDT reunion rides. As far as items that belonged to Tom Clark: there was one of his ISDT helmets, an ISDT T-shirt from Czechoslovakia, a single Hagan rear shock that had an inspection paint mark on it, aluminum water bottles, a couple of books signed to Tom Clark from Bud Ekins and Dick Mann, and a box of stickers. Additionally, there were some original maps to the 1973 ISDT hosted by the USA. I went through it all and took pictures to share with the members of the Leroy Winters Memorial ISDT Reunion Ride Facebook Group. The group was very helpful and excited about the photos I was posting.

Now that I had Jim Simmons' bike in my possession and a load of stuff to go through and research, I figured I better call him and set up a time to meet. Jim lived in Farmington, Missouri, which was only thirty minutes south of me. After all the grueling research I completed on the Harley-Davidson MX team bike, I had to take advantage of having all my answers in one spot with one visit with Jim—or so I thought.

I called Jim, and we agreed on a date about a month out. Leading up to the visit with Jim, I tried to pull together as much information as I could off the internet to share and to form questions to ask during the interview. At this point, I was still questioning the bike being the actual bike he raced in Austria and its whole back story after the 1976 ISDT. My goal was to put the Husqvarna back into racing condition—how it was during the Austria ISDT—so I had to figure out everything that had happened to it since then.

Meeting Jim

*T*he day came for me to visit Jim. I loaded up the bike, Jim's toolbox, and the box of extra parts I'd received from Johnny Waller. I figured by going through these items with Jim, it might jog his memory. A lot of time had obviously passed since the 1970s, and I wasn't sure just how much he would remember. On entering Farmington, the route to Jim's house took me past a good donut bakery, so I stopped in to grab some for our meeting. As I pulled into Jim's driveway, I was getting nervous and curious as to how all this was going to go. I rang the doorbell, and Jim answered. He looked just like an older version of the pictures I've seen of him on the internet. Jim was a tall man, well-built, and had a deep, commanding voice. He welcomed me in and introduced me to his wife, Joyce. She took the donuts from me and asked if I'd like some coffee. We headed over to the kitchen table where Jim and I sat across from each other. I started by introducing myself and giving a little bit of information about my motorcycle history. Joyce brought me over some coffee and joined us, and we all enjoyed the donuts I'd brought.

After we got through the introductions, Joyce went off to look for photos and newspaper clippings of Jim while I started going over my notes and questions. I talked about the preservation of the #49 Harley-Davidson team bike I was performing and how my plans were to do the same with his Husqvarna. I had my list of questions ready. First off, I wanted to learn more about Jim. I apologized that I never heard of him up until a few months earlier and explained how I came across his bike, which led me to the path that got me here. I learned Tom Reeves ("Craz"), who Johnny bought the bike from, actually worked with Jim at Flat River Glass Company. Jim was his supervisor in the maintenance department. Craz was the best welder on Jim's team. He was a Navy veteran and learned to weld while serving our country. Jim and Craz always talked motorcycles, and Jim gave Craz his Husqvarna years ago because of his passion for motorcycles. Once Jim was done with racing in the late 1970s, he was done. He gave away or sold off his bikes, consisting of a couple of Rokons and his Husqvarna. Jim also had a truckload of trophies he gave away as well. Craz was the recipient of many of Jim's trophies. Jim only kept a few trophies, which he said he'd show me later. Jim went to Craz's funeral, which was just a couple of months prior to our meeting. And he told me that when he did, that's when this curiosity started up in the back of his mind about what happened to his Husqvarna. It was kind of interesting how the bike came into my possession just a couple of weeks after Craz passed away. Jim knew Johnny Waller, as well. Johnny worked at the same company as Jim and Craz, but Jim did not realize that Johnny was into motorcycles. With the

Tom Reeves, or Craz as he was known. Photo by Dennis Degonia

dots now traced from Jim to the Husqvarna to me, I asked Jim where it all started for him. When did he start riding?

Jim started telling me about how he got into motorcycles. He and his friend Stan Rubottom grew up together in Esther, Missouri. They were childhood friends. They both went to the same grade school and high school, playing the same sports. During their junior year at Esther, they were both awarded the co-winners of the best all-around athlete award. During their senior year, they were both co-captains on the basketball, baseball, and track teams. After graduation, they both attended junior college, playing on the basketball team from 1960–62. After graduating from junior college in 1962, Stan got a job at McDonnel Douglas Aircraft in St. Louis, Missouri, while Jim went to Southeast Missouri State University to obtain his teaching degree. After one year of working, Stan quit his job at McDonnel Douglas and headed back to school at Southeast Missouri State with Jim. They both graduated two years later, in 1965, with teaching degrees. Jim taught at Bonne Terre and North County school districts after that, while Stan landed a teaching job at Festus and then North County.

Jim said they were really into water skiing, and they would ski at a lake in Mine La Motte, building their own ski ramps and slalom courses and skiing all the time. This area was surrounded by wide open riding areas, so they decided to try out motorcycle riding one day. At the time, recreational off-road motorcycle riding was really taking off in the United

STANLEY RUBOTTOM--
Co-Winner of Best All-
Around Athlete
JIM SIMMONS--Co-
Winner of Best All-Around
Athlete, President of Stu-
dent Body, Best All-Around
Student Award, Basketball
Free Throw Trophy

CAPTAIN JIM SIMMONS

JAMES EDWARD SIMMONS
Captain of Basketball Team,
Track, Baseball, Dramatics,
Student Body President, Presi-
dent of Student Council, Class
Pres., Beta Theta, Junior Play,
Senior Benefit Play, Escort in
Galleon Coronation, Escort in
Basketball Coronation.

CAPTAIN JIM SIMMONS

STANLEY RAY RUBOTTOM
Captain of Basketball Team,
Track, Baseball, Beta Theta,
Escort in Galleon Coronation,
Escort in Basketball Coronation.

CAPTAIN STAN RUBOTTOM

(Top) Jim and Stan: junior year co-winners of best all-around athletes.
(Left) Jim and Stan graduated top of their class in sports. Photos by Jim Simmons

States. They both went to Donelson Cycles in Flat River, Missouri, and bought Yamaha 80cc motorcycles. After about two months, they decided they needed something bigger, so they traded in their 80cc bikes for Yamaha 125cc dirt bikes. Now they felt like they had some real bikes. Their first brush with competitive racing came at a race near High Ridge, Missouri. This is where they were first exposed to the Husqvarna motorcycle. Their competitive nature drove them to move up to Husqvarnas after that.

A visit to Dave Mungenast's dealership off Gravois Avenue in St. Louis was in order. While there, they both purchased Husqvarnas—and became friends with Dave Mungenast while doing so. Dave opened St. Louis Honda Motorcycles at 6820 Gravois in St. Louis in March of 1965. Dave was a business owner and an off-road motorcycle racer. In 1967, Dave was chosen to race in the Poland ISDT for the USA Vase Team with the likes of John Penton, Malcolm Smith, Bud Ekins, and Leroy Winters—all riding Husqvarnas. This was Dave's first of nine ISDTs he would compete in. Dave became a Husqvarna dealer in 1969. It wasn't until meeting Dave that Jim and Stan had ever even heard of the ISDT.

• • •

*I*n 1969, when Jim and Stan were both twenty-seven years old and interested in competitive off-road racing with their newly purchased Husqvarnas, they could not have had a better place to practice than the property of St. Joseph Lead Company. Both Jim and Stan's fathers worked there, and so did Jim's grandpa. Jim and Stan were among the first to ever ride on that property. Once the St. Joseph Lead Company shut down in 1972, they still went there daily to get their fix. What is now called St. Joe Park—the place where I first rode—was then called #9 hill due to the corresponding #9 mine shaft in the area. Jim said that he and Stan rode out at St. Joe Park back before it was ever a park. Because Jim and Stan had family that worked for the company, they had unlimited access to thousands of riding acres. I guess you could say that Jim and Stan are the fore-riders of St. Joe Park. A couple of riding friends, Wayne Gibson and Greg White, would join them in their excursions. In the mid-1970s, they were part of a group of riders that pushed to turn the property into today's off-road riding park.

In 1975, three years after it shut down, St. Joseph Lead Company donated twenty-five buildings of their largest mine-mill complex, and the surrounding land, to the Missouri Department of Natural Resources. The city of Flat River held a town hall meeting to discuss what to do with it. Jim said, "The meeting was split into two groups. You had the equestrians and the off-road motorcyclers." Representing the motorcyclers were the main motorcycle dealership owners in the area, such as Mungenast, Donelson, and Surdyke. And Gary Surdyke, owner of Surdyke Yamaha in Festus, Missouri, showed up with none other than motocross superstar Bob Hannah. Bob was in town competing in the Cycle World USA Trans-AMA race in St. Peters and was staying at Gary's house. For Bob to attend the meeting with Gary, was a real demonstration of his dedication to the sport. That meeting helped determine what St. Joe Park is today, one of the biggest off-road riding parks in Southeast Missouri.

• • •

Within a year, Jim and Stan started racing enduros all across the U.S.: Potosi, Missouri, always hosted the "Busted Piston" Enduro; Lansing, Michigan, hosted the Big Jack Pine Enduro; Shelby, Indiana, hosted the Burr Oak Enduro; Lake Hope, Ohio, hosted the Little Burr Enduro; and Dalton, Georgia, hosted the Stone Mountain Enduro—these were just a few they raced in. Wayne Gibson and Greg White would join them when they could. All this traveling to gain A-rider status took a lot of time, and with Jim and Stan's teaching jobs, something had to go.

Jim and Stan both decided to quit their teaching jobs to dedicate more time to racing. In today's world, you would think these guys were crazy to pursue an impossible dream at their ages. But, if you put yourself in the early 1970s, when off-road motorcycle racing was exploding, you would understand that Jim and Stan had the chance at something great. The movie *On*

Any Sunday had just hit the theaters, and people everywhere were eager to compete for the highest achievement in off-road racing, to be selected to the USA ISDT Team. To have the flexibility to take off at will—and to be able to afford to—they both started working for Brown Carpet in Esther, Missouri. Working for Brown Carpet also exposed them to physical labor, which kept them in shape. More on Jim and Stan's ISDT adventures to come.

• • •

At one point during our meet and greet, Jim stood up and said, "Let me show you something in the basement." Jim had a storage room where he kept memorabilia from his riding days. The first thing I noticed was his three prized trophies. The

Buddy Greg White and his Penton. Photo by Jim Simmons

first was a trophy from when Jim won the B-Medium Weight Class at the 1971 Jack Pine National Endurance Race, which advanced him to A-Rider level status. Jim said that during that race, he was on the same line as Ron Bohn, an A-Rider at the time, so all he had to do was keep pace, and he'd have it made. Bohn was the National Enduro champion that year.

I later came across *The Daily Journal* newspaper article about that race and it read:

Jim Simmons of Esther was the winner of the medium weight division in the 44th annual Jack Pine National Motorcycle Endurance race at Lake Houghton, Michigan, over the past weekend. Over 600 entries from every state in the union and one foreign country competed in the 420-mile endurance event that was on Saturday and Sunday. To be eligible for Sunday's final session of the race, riders on Saturday had to average 24 miles per hour over a distance of 236 miles through a wooded course. Two other residents, Stan Rubottom and Greg White of

Desloge, also participated in the race.[7]

The second trophy was from the May 1973 Burr Oak Enduro, where Jim was the Heavy Weight Champion, riding on a Husqvarna. No story went along with the Burr Oak trophy, but it did strike up a conversation about Jim winning the 1972 Little Burr Enduro on May 28, 1972, where he was the A-Class Medium Weight Champion. At the 1972 Little Burr, both Jim and Tom Penton were on the same line. Jim stayed right with Tom the entire race, and they both won their respective classes. Both Jim and Tom became good friends that day, which would lead Tom to visit Jim down the road and riding at #9 hill.

Jim Hollander photographed in Austria, 1976. Photo by Tony Budde

The third trophy was a club team award he won with Stan and Jim Hollander at the Berkshire two-day trial in October 1972. This trial was a precursor to the 1973 ISDT that the United States would be hosting. A *Cycle News* article on the event stated: Club team award went to St. Louis Honda riders Rubottom, Simmons and Hollander. Strangely, they were on two Husqvarnas and a Penton.[8]

Later on, Jim would be teammates with Hollander again, but on team Rokon. Jim Hollander has quite a colorful racing history. He started out racing enduros on his Penton motorcycle, where he caught the eye of founder John Penton. He got a job working for Penton and started his ISDT racing at the 1972 Czechoslovakia ISDT for team Canada. In 1973, he raced the ISDT in Dalton, Massachusetts, riding a Penton. Hollander would then switch to Rokon, and compete in the 1974, 1975, and 1976 ISDTs. Hollander

Jim Simmons' Hallman riding gloves given to him by Lars Larsson. Photo by Keith Geisner

also gave Rokon their only overall win at the Rome City, Michigan, two-day qualifier in 1976.

Next, Jim pulled a pair of riding gloves and a white helmet down from the shelf. He told me that I could "take them home for now." The gloves were Hallman brand, a gift from Lars Larsson (another ISDT legend), and the white helmet—the story behind that blew me away.

Along with the gloves and helmet, he gave me a St. Louis Honda jersey, St. Louis Dirt Bike

Headquarters Husqvarna lightweight jacket, and a Cycle East Husqvarna jersey. Jim wasn't sure what he wanted to do with his trophies and a Cycle East helmet he had, so those stayed put. I was in shock and honored to be given what items he did give me; I was not expecting this to happen. With my hands full, we turned the lights off and we headed back upstairs to go outside and see the Husqvarna. Jim said he'd tell me more about the gloves and white helmet in a bit.

Jim and I walked out to my truck, where his ISDT Husqvarna waited patiently. Once I had the bike unloaded, Jim walked around it and examined its condition. Jim confirmed that it was his bike, and he pointed out that there was no serial number on the frame.

Jim and I went through the toolbox I'd received with the bike. He'd pick up a part and tell me a story about how it broke a lot. Jim didn't believe he raced the bike after the 1976 ISDT, but there just seemed to be too many extra parts for him not to have ridden it more. He said his nephew took it for a week to do some trail riding, but that was it. I'd find out more later. The only major thing that was missing on the bike was the number plates. Jim thought they might be at his lake house in Arkansas, but he wasn't 100 percent sure. At this time, I showed him Tom Clark's ISDT helmet, and Jim said he still had his USA helmet, too. And he said I could have it, but it was also in Arkansas. Jim said Tom was a good man and was a very good rider, and it was thanks to him that the Fort Hood, Texas two-day qualifier came to be. While visiting Fort Hood—to sell them on the Rokon motorcycle—the base commander, whose son also rode motorcycles off-road, became interested. So the qualifier was created right then and there to show the military how good the Rokon motorcycle was. I found this information very interesting, and I took this opportunity to ask Jim how he received the Husqvarna.

I discussed earlier how Rokon went out of business in 1976, the same year Jim was racing for the Rokon team and qualified for the ISDT. With the company now bankrupt, Jim was without a bike and team support. I found an article in *Cycle News* that summed up the situation and hinted at how Jim received his Husqvarna:

Apparently not feeling too let down by the Rokon factory's withdrawal of support (riders were furnished with bikes and parts, at no expense), Jim Simmons, thirty-three-year-old carpet installer for Brown Carpet Co. offers special thanks to Marty Ray, Rokon's head wrench and to Rokon, Inc. Still, he needed some help and found it with Husqvarna through his friend Ed Schmidt. "Ed came over and helped me build a new bike," Jim added.[9]

• • •

Ed Schmidt, the East Coast National Parts Manager for Husqvarna, hooked Jim up with his ISDT Husqvarna. Ed was also a damn good off-road rider himself. Ed became friends with Dave Mungenast around 1965, and when Dave started selling Husqvarnas, Ed bought one of the first to arrive at St. Louis Honda. Ed qualified for the ISDT in 1970 and 1971 through 1975. He was part of the Silver Vase winning team of the 1973 ISDT hosted by the USA. Before Ed became a serious off-road racer, he was competing in hill climbs around White City, Peoria, and Mattoon, Illinois.

Ed was the overall winner of the Black Coal Enduro in 1972. But it wouldn't have happened without a little help from Jim. Ed's VDO speedo broke, and he couldn't keep time. Ed was about two minutes ahead of Jim—and then Jim caught up. Jim said he rode up on Ed messing with his speedo and his watch. Jim ended up running point for Ed and helped him finish. The Black Coal was close to Evansville, Indiana, and was managed by Jerry Schuler, who was good friends with Ed Schmidt.

Before Ed became the East Coast National Parts Manager for Husqvarna, none other than John Penton held that title (but the distribution center was in Loraine, Ohio, at that time). Ed became manager once it relocated to Nashville, Tennessee. Due to Ed's excellent riding history with Husqvarna, he was an ideal candidate for the role. To bring his history full circle with Dave Mungenast, Ed would host training class and warranty services, where he would teach everyone how to work on Husqvarnas at Dave's St. Louis Cycle & Van Accessories business location. Ed had his own room for this. Dave set it up to where Ed could work for Husqvarna and still handle Mungenast parts. Ed would return to St. Louis and go to work for Dave as an office manager once he left Husqvarna

So, how did Ed Schmidt come through for Jim? He told Jim to come down to the Eastern Husqvarna distribution center in Nashville. Jim was pretty excited; he pictured a nice new Husqvarna all setup and ready to go. He grabbed his tiedown straps and headed south to retrieve his new bike. When he arrived, he got a big surprise. Ed invited him in, grabbed a shopping cart, and said, "Follow me." He started going down the aisles, pulling parts off the shelf needed to build the bike. Jim was shaking his head and laughing while telling me this story. He never guessed he'd be building a bike from scratch, but he was! And, boy, was he thankful. So, the frame of Jim's bike does not have a vehicle identification number (VIN) stamped on it because it was never sold to the public. I never would have guessed. With a newly assembled bike, and after getting sponsored by the Lubbock Trail Riders from Lubbock, Texas, Jim was ready to go.

Jim really looked up to Ed, who not only knew his stuff, but was a real character. One time in the early 1970s, Jim asked Ed, "Why is my Husky so hard to start after falling over?" Ed replied, "Don't fall over!" Stan Rubottom's version of the story goes that Jim asked Ed why his Husky loads up all the time, and Ed replied, "You aren't riding it hard enough!" The three riders spent a lot of time together. This leads to another story when they were headed out West to a qualifier. It was Stan, Jim, and Ed. Ed was driving and took a wrong turn after Kansas City and didn't realize it until they showed up at the Oklahoma state border.

• • •

I asked Jim what the story was behind the Cycle East jersey, and he said it was a company that sold riding gear and accessories. They sent Jim a helmet and gear and said he could order whatever he wanted out of their catalog, as long as he wore their brand. Jim said he couldn't remember ordering much of anything. Later on, this Cycle East jersey would help me answer some questions that came up during the preservation of Jim's Husqvarna—more on that later.

(Top left) The front of Jim's St. Louis Dirt Bike Headquarters Husqvarna lightweight jacket. (Top right) The back of Jim's St. Louis Dirt Bike Headquarters Husqvarna lightweight jacket. (Bottom left) The front of Jim's St. Louis Honda jersey. (Bottom right) The back of Jim's St. Louis Honda jersey. Photos by Keith Geisner

Reuniting Jim with his Husqvarna. Photo by Keith Geisner

Before we said our goodbyes, Jim agreed to take some photos with me next to his bike with Tom Clark's ISDT helmet next to it.

Before leaving, Jim gave me three books: *Malcolm! The Autobiography* by Malcolm Smith with Mitch Boehm, *Take It to the Limit: The Dave Mungenast Way* written by Ed Youngblood, and *Mann of His Time*, another book written by Ed Youngblood. I would read these books for inspiration while completing the final stages of Harley-Davidson MX bike preservation.

As I drove away, I reflected on what I'd discovered about the Husqvarna in the back of my truck. Jim Simmons' Husqvarna was never meant to be. It was not a production-line motorcycle. It did not roll off the assembly line, get crated, and shipped to America. It was assembled from a bunch of new Husqvarna parts. These parts were replacement parts designated to fix or repair several other motorcycles. Some of these parts could have been for last year's model, for a different size motorcycle, or a motorcycle used for motocross versus enduros.

Because of Jim and Ed, these parts came together. They were hand-selected by the East Coast Husqvarna parts manager Ed Schmidt, a four-time ISDT qualifier, and 1972 Black Coal overall winner. To say Ed knew what parts to grab is an understatement. He chose parts based on his experience and knowledge, not only as a rider but as an experienced Husqvarna employee. Assembled by both Jim and Ed, an off-road racing weapon to compete in the 1976 Austria ISDT was built with precision and care.

For this bike to now be around today is quite incredible. It crossed the ocean as hundreds of individual parts from Sweden and was then assembled into a motorcycle in Nashville, Tennessee, only to be shipped back across the ocean to race in Austria. Then, after being thrashed for six straight days, it was shipped across the ocean for a third time to Farmington, Missouri. It exchanged ownership four times until finding me in 2017, forty-one years later. You cannot make this stuff up. This bike was born from a bunch of parts. Because of a chain of events—Rokon closing its doors, Ed Schmidt helping out Jim Simmons, Jim giving the bike to his friend Craz, Johnny Waller buying the bike from Craz, and me making an offer on a 1978 YZ400 Yamaha, the bike is now in my possession to be preserved for all to see for generations to come. When you get an opportunity like this, you do not think twice about it. You put the time in and give it the respect it deserves.

Jim and his newly assembled ride for the 1976 ISDT. Photo by the Schmidt Collection

Ed Schmidt at the 1973 ISDT. Photo by Jim Simmons

Jim's Cycle East jersey. Photo by Keith Geisner

The Mexican ISDT Team

*T*he white helmet Jim gave me had green and red pinstripes and the flag of Mexico on its left side. I saw that Jim qualified and took a silver in the 1978 ISDT in Sweden, but I was unaware that he did it riding for the Mexican team. It just so happens 1978 was the first year for the Mexico team to participate in the ISDT. The story goes like this: Jim just missed out on qualifying for the ISDT that year. He got a call a few days later from fellow ISDT rider and friend Lars Larsson. Lars asked Jim if he would want to ride in the ISDT, and Jim said, "Well, yes, but how, we both didn't qualify?" Lars told Jim he had friends in Mexico who could hook them up with an address and identification if they wanted to represent Mexico at the 1978 ISDT in Sweden. You see, Lars was originally from Sweden, so being able to participate in the 1978 ISDT was very important to him. So, Jim, along with fellow rider Fred Cameron, joined Lars in representing Mexico. The helmet Jim gave me was the first-ever Mexico ISDT helmet that Bell had made.

Jim holding his Team Mexico 1978 ISDT helmet present day. Photo by Keith Geisner

A 1978 article in the *American Motorcyclist* said it best:

After failing to qualify for the 37-man U.S. squad, a trio of resourceful Yanks—Lars Larsson, Fred Cameron and Jim Simmons—suddenly appeared as the Moto Club DaValle, riding for Mexico! (Since Larsson was a former Trophy Team member of Sweden, the questionable nature of their entry was "overlooked" by the organizing Swedes.) Larsson struck gold, while Cameron and Simmons slipped off the pace for silver medals. Resplendent in its sombreros, the team wound up 16th place.[10]

At the opening ceremony, Jim said all three of them wore sombreros and a blanket draped across their chests to represent Mexico. When other Spanish-speaking countries approached them, they knew their cover was blown, as none of them spoke Spanish. It was then that Jim showed me photos of the first-ever Mexico ISDT team in their riding gear, helmets, and sombreros. I noticed the helmet Jim gave me was missing its visor and figured I'd find one for it later. The missing Hallman visor and Jim's current Hallman riding gloves also came from Lars Larsson.

Lars Larsson was a pioneer motocross rider and off-road racer from Sweden who helped introduce motocross racing to America in the late 1960s. He was the leading ISDT rider during the 1960s and 1970s. He earned multiple gold medals riding for the United States, Mexico, and his native Sweden. In addition to his excellent racing record, Lars was also instrumental in setting up the original Husqvarna dealership network across the U.S. in the late 1960s, which helped further off-road racing here. He also helped launch Torsten Hallman Original Racewear (THOR), which became a leading motocross racing gear and apparel company.

I was lucky enough to speak to Lars about how the Mexico team came to be. In 1978, Lars was too busy racing in California to travel and compete in the two-day reliability trials. He pleaded with Al Eames, AMA ISDT manager, to see if he could still be invited on the USA team. The 1978 ISDT was special to Lars since it was hosted by his home country of Sweden. Lars did not receive good news from Al, so he took it upon himself to do something about it. Lars called down to the Mexican Federation and told them he wanted to form a Mexican ISDT team and needed three licenses. They told him to come on down, so Lars flew down to Mexico City, paid for the licenses, and formed the 1978 Mexican ISDT team.

When I asked Lars how he chose Jim for the team, he said, "That's a hell of a good question. I have no clue." He knew Fred better than Jim because they both lived in California, and they camped out a few times, but he could not remember why he picked Jim. He later said that it was because he knew that Jim, Fred, and himself were all crazy enough to do it. Lars first confirmed both Jim and Fred were game before going to Mexico to get the licenses…and the rest is history.

In 1979, Lars and Carl Cranke were pre-running the Baja 1000. They got into the town of San Felipe and went out to eat. While eating, they started a conversation with a group of Mexican motorcyclists. They asked what their names were and when they heard Lars state his name, their eyes lit up. They said, "Are you the first Mexican to ride Six-Days?" Lars nodded with a smile, and that started a bond and big friendship between him and motorcyclists all over Mexico.

The third member of the 1978 Mexico team was Fred Cameron. Fred, a dentist by trade, was no stranger to off-road racing. After finishing up his U.S. Navy active duty in Corte Madera, California, some neighbor kids showed him what a dirt bike could do and, after seeing the movie *On Any Sunday*, he was hooked.

At the age of twenty-eight, a patient of Fred's traded him a motorcycle for a crown, and he turned around and traded that in for a 1970 250 Suzuki Savage, a two-stroke enduro bike. He learned a little about riding and wanted to try an enduro in Northern California. Fred

Lars Larsson, Jim Simmons, and Fred Cameron. Team Mexico 1978 ISDT. Photo by Jim Simmons

Lars Larsson, Jim Simmons, and Fred Cameron. Team Mexico at the opening ceremony of the 1978 ISDT. Photo by Fred Cameron

realized that he was neither fast nor very good, but he had the desire, the endurance, and was a finisher. His next bike was a Bultaco Alpina, which taught him some trials skills but no speed skills. After his first two-day qualifier in Oregon, he realized he should never try a two-day qualifier again. But, the more time that passed and the more he thought about it, he was sure the problem was the bike and not him. So, he bought a Penton 175. A friend of his had just returned from the 1973 ISDT that took place in America. He showed Fred all the pictures, and his gold medal, and, at that point, Fred knew he had to make this his goal.

In 1974, Fred bought a 250 Penton and rode several qualifiers, and finished about fiftieth to qualify for the 1974 ISDT in Italy. He found out that Canada was taking some qualified U.S. riders to fill out their team. Fred joined Dave Mungenast as Canadian riders to compete in the ISDT hosted by Italy. Fred's bike broke at the end of the fourth day, but his body and spirit did not. He would continue to qualify every year through 1979. In 1975, he rode the Isle of Man ISDT for Canada and won a bronze medal. In 1976, he qualified as first alternate for the Austria ISDT. When he arrived at the start along with five other alternates, none of them got to ride. The AMA forgot to send their names to preregistration, but Fred managed to ride every day as a pre rider and chase rider. In 1978, he won a silver medal while teaming with Jim and Lars at the Swedish ISDT, representing the first Mexican team. The following year, he would team up with Lars and Barry Higgins to race for Mexico—again at the 1979 ISDT in Germany, earning a bronze medal. The Mexican team was awarded the Wattling trophy in Germany for most improved and inspiring team. Fred would round out his career with Mexico by competing in the 1984 ISDE event hosted by Holland, where he would collect another bronze. Then, in 1990, Fred would represent Mexico for the last time, where it all began: in Sweden. Fred would hour out on the third day.

When I asked Fred what he thought the most interesting part of representing Mexico in 1978 was, he said, "Lars pulling off the event. No one thought we could do it, unsure we would ride. The AMA was livid and swore that we would be removed. At the protest meeting, the jury called to discuss the situation. Lars and his friend, who was the organizer of the event, were there and just told the AMA to sit down. We were admitted, and his decision was final. The AMA vowed it would never happen again, but of course, it did several more times. Now, they've changed the rule to state that you need a passport for proof."

The first time Fred met Jim was at the 1978 ISDT in Sweden. He said, "Jim was a relaxed, slow talker, but confident about his abilities and could back it up with his riding."

The 1980 Mexico ISDT team actually had Mexicans on it. It was hosted by France that year. From 1980 till today, Mexico has entered a team to compete in the ISDT/ISDE and it all started with Lars Larsson.

Lars Larsson, Fred Cameron, and Barry Higgins. Team Mexico 1979 ISDT. Photo by Lars Larsson

Lars Larsson and Team Mexico 1980 ISDT. Photo by Lars Larsson

Lars Larsson, Jim Simmons, and Fred Cameron. Team Mexico 1978 ISDT. Photo by Jim Simmons.

The Mungenast Influence

In March 2018, Ray Mungenast and Dave Larsen allowed me to show my #49 Harley-Davidson motocross team bike at the Mungenast Classic Automobiles & Motorcycles Museum during their Supercross party. I just finished reading Ray's father's book, *Take It to the Limit: The Dave Mungenast Way*. To say I was inspired was an understatement. I should have read the book years earlier, but it took meeting Jim to make it happen. Now that I had, it was even more of an honor to be at the museum. I reached out to Jim and Stan to see if they wanted to attend. At that point, I still hadn't met Stan, but I knew they were both friends with the Mungenasts. I also wanted to show Jim my preservation work on the Harley-Davidson (which, as you know, I was planning to do with his Husqvarna). After getting the Harley-Davidson set up in the front room of the museum, Jim and Stan arrived. You could tell the two of them together were trouble. Ray and Dave were there, as well. It was a treat to have them all in one place and to listen to their stories. Dave Larsen, Mungenast's longest-standing employee of over fifty-five years is the guy who sold Jim and Stan their first Husqvarnas after they quit riding Yamahas. They both purchased the sportsman models, which, at first, didn't start out good—they battled constant electrical issues—but, eventually, it got worked out. "The bikes just weren't of the same caliber as Jim and Stan," Dave had said. But, because of this mishap, Dave, Jim, and Stan became great friends, attending enduros together and bench racing whenever they would meet up. I was blown away by how many stories they had, and I could tell there was more to their friendship than just having Dave Sr. in common. Jim is full of stories, and an excellent storyteller.

That day at the museum, one story stood out.

Jim, Dave Sr., Dave Jr., Ray, Ed Schmidt, and a few other regulars went riding one day in Potosi. This was in 1975, and it was the dead of winter, and the ground was frozen. All was going well until they came upon a frozen water hole they had to go around. Dave Jr. was, coincidentally, test riding a customer's bike that afternoon. When he attempted to maneuver around the water hole, the bike slid out and hit a cedar tree. In the process, a branch must have yanked the fuel line off the petcock. Fuel started splashing onto the exhaust and sparkplug, igniting the fumes. Everyone jumped off their bikes to help put the fire out, but there was no stopping it once the magnesium motor ignited. The bike burned to the ground.

Jeff Oakes—the owner of that bike—still remembers the phone call he received from Dave Sr. like it was yesterday. The conversation went like this:

"Hey, Jeff, this is Dave."

"Hi, Dave, how are you doing?"

"Well…I got good news, and I got bad news".

"What's the good news?" Jeff asked.

"Oh, well, we got your bike running like a champ. You would've really liked it. But that gets me to the bad news. It was really cold out, and I'm not sure what happened, but your bike caught on fire. We tried to put the fire out. There was a creek nearby, so we took our riding jackets off and soaked them in water to smother the fire, but the thing just kept burning and burning due to the magnesium engine. You might want to come down and take a look at your bike."

Jeff drove down to the shop. He said the bike looked like a melted marshmallow. Dave, being the way he was, had already prepped a brand-new replacement bike for him. Dave said, "I know this one runs right. We'll figure out something to do with the burnt one."

Jeff said he's probably told that story nine million times over the last forty years. It was one of many great experiences with Dave, who, as everyone says, was a real gentleman. Jeff bought a ton of bikes from Dave and is still a Husqvarna nut.

It was Dave who originally got Jeff into motorcycles.

Back in 1965, Jeff was walking down Gravois Road, feeling down from a recent fight with his wife. He came upon Dirt Bike Headquarters, and they had a bike hanging by wires in the window. He walked in and met Dave Mungenast. And, within two hours, Dave sold him a Montesa Lacrosse. When Jeff got home with the bike, it was the last straw for the wife. They were divorced a year later, but Jeff never looked back. He was hooked on motorcycles. Jeff told Dave, "If you hadn't caught my attention with the dirt bike in the window, I might have never discovered motorcycles." Jeff wasn't the only person who Dave Mungenast had influenced throughout the years. His kindness has affected many great names in the sport, Lars Larsson being one of them.

When talking with Lars Larsson about his Mexico ISDT team, I also asked about his history with Dave Mungenast. Lars said, "I was very close friends with Dave Mungenast. The first year I spent in the United States, my first home was with John Penton, my second home was with Leroy Winters, and my third home was with Dave Mungenast in St. Louis. Dave guided us through some of our business ventures when we were new to this world and more naïve. Dave was our mentor. He helped us when we had our business, Torsten Hallman Racing."

Lars had a story of Dave's hospitality from racing in the 1967 Inter-AM series. "In 1967, when Joel Robert and Roger De Coster were here doing the Inter-AM, we raced them in Sedan, Kansas. The CZ guys beat the hell out of us, so we figured we had to do something with our bikes. We went to Dave Mungenast's shop on Gravois Road and asked him if we could pit in his service area and work on them, and Dave said, 'Of course!' We took our cylinders off and we were going to file a little here and a little there. On a Husky, the liner sticks out on the bottom of the cylinder. There's an opening for the transfer port, and there's like a little bridge there. My teammate, Ake Johnson, dropped his cylinder on the floor and broke that bridge off on one side. Ake picked up the cylinder, turned to us, and said, 'It's better to make it even, huh?' Then, Ake picked up a hammer and broke off the other bridge. So, then he didn't have any bridges!" Lars said, "Those were our factory bikes! And everyone thought we were on exquisite bikes. Well, that's how factory bikes were!"

• • •

Dave Mungenast not only sold motorcycles in the St. Louis area, but he also gave people a place to ride. Dave opened Pacific Cycle Playground after opening St. Louis Honda Motorcycles in 1965. Honda encouraged dealerships to own property where customers could ride their product. Honda stated that dealers should invest in areas for people to ride. That way, the dealership could sell the motorcycle, give customers a place to enjoy riding, and they could come back for replacement parts—kind of a closed loop marketing strategy. Dave Larsen said that Ed Viermann was the mastermind behind the trail system. Ed's photo was on the flyer for Pacific Cycle Playground. He would be the man behind the trails laid out in the Potosi area for the ISDT two-day qualifiers.

Over time, the Pacific Cycle Playground became too small, and a bigger location needed to be sourced. That's when Dave opened Doe Run Cycle Park in 1970. The 1700-acre cycle park had a MX track, miles of off-road trails, and a big pavilion. It was a first-class setup. Pacific Cycle Playground was small in comparison to Doe Run Cycle Park. In order to promote the Doe Run Cycle Park, Dave Larsen created the Doe Run Enduro Team, which was a sanctioned AMA club. They would hold annual enduros and motocross races. Doe Run Cycle Park was unique because they had closed-course events, which allowed kids under sixteen to compete.

The terrain that Doe Run Cycle Park provided was very rocky, which drew a lot of attention from the professional off-road riders. Penton, Burleson, and Mann are just a few names that would test and train at the park. And, since Dave owned the park, Honda used it for pre-production testing of its motorcycles, which included the famous first-generation Honda CR Elsinore. Ray Mungenast remembers it clearly. He was too small to ride the Elsinore during the testing, but his older brother, Dave Jr., was not. Honda had two or three of each CR model there with mechanics checking engine and shock temperatures after each ride, validating vibration issues, and so on. Ray was riding his Honda XR75, viewing the action during the heavy product testing.

Not only did Doe Run Cycle Park provide a place for people to ride their motorcycles, but they would also hold motocross training classes there. Rolf Tibblin held a motocross school and physical training course at the park a couple of times. Ray had the opportunity to attend. Rolf was Swedish and a three-time motocross world champion who focused on physical fitness. Physical training classes would be held at the Ironton High School gym. It included calisthenics, stretches, and strengthening exercises. In the afternoon, training would take place on the motocross track at the park. Anyone into motocross in the area would attend.

Pat Hagerty Sr. lived at the park and managed it for Dave. Doe Run Cycle Park was in operation from 1970 to 1980. Pat Sr.'s son, Pat Jr., would eventually go to work for Dave Mungenast and would go on to become the district service rep for Honda's motorcycle division.

Pat Jr. was a very good MX racer, as well. More on the Hagerty family later.

• • •

*I*t was at the 2017 Mungenast Museum Supercross party when I first met Ray Mungenast. I didn't know how to approach Ray, so I went up to him and started a conversation about his mother's beautiful sculptures; she was a well-known local artist. That lead to motorcycles and the rest is history. When I first learned of the Jim Simmons' Husqvarna, Ray was one of the first people I contacted. Ray's family history in off-road motorcycle racing and sales is quite impressive.

Dave Mungenast Sr. had three sons, Dave Jr., Ray, and Kurt. Ray was the middle child and the one who followed his father's footsteps when it came to racing Six Days. Even before Ray graduated high school, he was competing in two-day qualifiers. No sooner had Ray graduated in 1979 than he was off competing full time to qualify. Ray was surrounded by this type of off-road racing his whole life. As a young boy, there were names like LeRoy Winters, Jack Penton, Lars Larsson, and Dick Burrelson staying at his family's house regularly. In 1981, Ray's efforts paid off when he became the youngest member of the USA ISDE team at the age of twenty. That year the hosting country was Italy. Ray would go on a five-year run of ISDE USA competition from 1981 through 1985 in the hosting

Dave Mungenast Jr. performing early Elsinore testing at Doe Run Cycle Park. Photo by the Mungenast Collection

countries of Italy, Czechoslovakia, Wales, Netherlands, and Spain, medaling in every event.

Because Ray was always around Dave Sr.'s riding friends, it was only a matter of time before he got to know their kids. Through interaction between his father and Jim Simmons, Ray got

DOE RUN
cycle park
1700 acres

OFF ROAD RIDING 1 HR. FROM ST. LOUIS

ACCOMODATIONS AND FACILITIES

- OPEN EVERY DAY
- AMPLE PARKING AREA
- SANITARY RESTROOM FACILITIES

- SHADED PICNIC AREAS
- PLAYGROUND FOR THE LITTLE ONES
- PRIVATE CAMPING SPOTS

- MILES OF TRAILS
- GAS-OIL AND SMALL PARTS
- A.T.V. AVAILABLE TO HAUL DISABLED BIKES

(Above) Original Doe Run Cycle Park brochure. (Next) Original Doe Run Cycle Park brochure. Photos by the Mungenast Collection

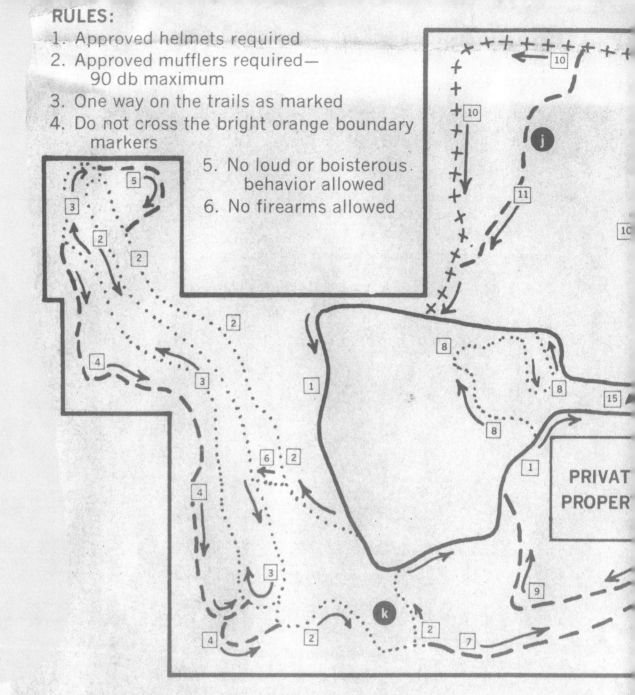

NOTE:

All trails marked in green for one way traffic and all return to headquarters *except* 3 5 8 9 marked green and red which could cause a continuous loop.

Trails are rated as follows:

· · · · · · · · · · · · · ·		— — — — — —		+ + + + + +	
EASY		**MEDIUM**		**DEMANDING**	
1 *	8	18	4	11	10
2	12	20	5	17	16
3	13	22	7	19	
6	14		9	21	
	15				

*NOTE: TRAIL 1 EASY

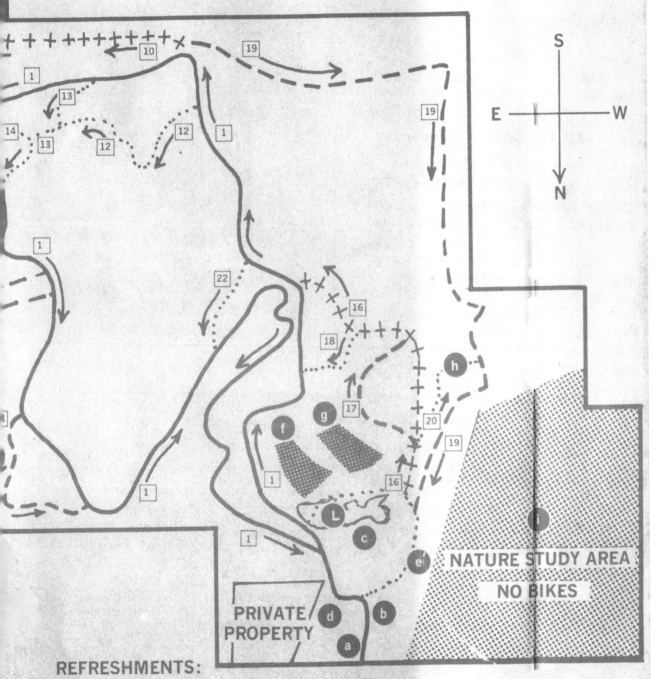

a. Entrance

b. Headquarters

c. Parking and activity field

d. Children's play area

e. Camping area

f. Mini-Bike area ▒▒▒

g. Beginner trail

h. Hill climb

i. Nature study area (no bikes)

j. Highest point in park—1,582 ft.

k. Pine Forest

L. Moto Cross course

NATURE STUDY AREA
NO BIKES

PRIVATE PROPERTY

REFRESHMENTS:

 Soda and sandwiches available at all times.

Trained first-aid personnel in attendance.

IF YOU CAN DO IT ON A MOTORCYCLE...
YOU CAN DO IT AT DOE RUN CYCLE PARK!

We invite you to visit the Ozark's only complete motorcycle playground and training area. 1,700 acres of privately owned land featuring riding areas of every type. Whether you're a racer or just a rider, a beginner or an expert, you'll truly enjoy Doe Run Cycle Park.

MOTOCROSS: Sharpen your motocross skills with the help of our .7 mile training track. Our jumps, switchbacks and off camber turns will make you a better racer . . . or make you quit!

TRIALS: If you're into trials, take on our ever changing sections. Designed by a 5 time medal winner of the International Six Day Trials. The beginner sections are designed to teach the skills of trials riding . . . the expert sections are designed to make you use those skills.

TRAIL RIDING:

Miles and miles of trail wind through the tall Ozark timber of Doe Run Cycle Park. Stay ''close in'' on beginner and family style trails or grab a seldom traveled track to the peace and solitude of the deep woods.

LAY AREAS:

you want to teach someone to ride or just let off a little
eam, our open riding areas, play hills and whoop-de-doos are
t for you.

PICNICING — CONCESSIONS

Bring your own family style
meals and enjoy an outdoor picnic
or use the covered shelter of our new
guest pavilion. If you'd rather buy it than bring
it, our newly completed concession facility can
feed the hearties appetites.

CAMPING

For our guests who want
to spend the night at
Doe Run . . . just pitch
your tent or park your
camper and slumber off
in the clean country air.

★Other Doe Run features include children's playground
equipment, gasoline, oil and small parts, sanitary
restrooms, ample parking and A.T.V. available
for disabled bike recovery.

(Previous, current) Original Doe Run Cycle Park brochure. Photo by the Mungenast Collection

to know and started dating Jim's daughter April. They were close in age and grew up together because of racing. Ray knew Jim and Stan very well and remembered the first time he took April on a date. It was during the winter of 1985. He pulled into the driveway at Jim's house around 6:30 in the evening. He noticed Jim's truck with Jim, Stan, and Robbie Harris sitting in it at the end of the yard. The three of them together were some characters and here they were hanging out in the middle of winter drinking beer in a parked truck. As Ray approached the front door, he heard a guy yell, "Hey, get over here." Ray walked over to the truck. Stan and Robbie were in there giggling, but Jim was not. Ray looked at Jim, and Jim said, "I just want to tell you that you're no different than anyone else who comes around here. She leaves with her pants on, and she comes home with her pants on." At that same moment, Stan and Robbie spit out their beer, busting out laughing. Meanwhile, Jim didn't crack a smile. Ray said, "Yep, I get it." That was the kind of relationship Jim and Ray had. Jim could be serious but he was also a jokester. Ray knew this and respected Jim. Ray and April had their childhood relationship and are still good friends today.

Through the years, Dave Sr.'s friends sort of took Ray under their wing. Even years after Jim quit racing, he would still show his support for Ray. The year Ray took second overall at the Flat River Grand Prix, Jim was there watching. He would visit with Ray in the pits and check-in. Ray looked up to Jim. He grew up watching this giant figure of a man race with the best of them through his Rokon, Husqvarna, and Yamaha days—just like he had with his father and all his father's friends. This inspired Ray to take his love of off-racing to the limit and pursue his dream of competing in the ISDE.

One interesting story stuck in Ray's memory. It was during a District 17 Mt. Olive Enduro in White City, Illinois. Ray was there as a spectator since he was too young to race. It was early in the morning. Not too far from the start, there was a bottleneck on a steep, slimy hill that was tight with trees. Riders were just all over the place, and people were backed up on the bottom, waiting for an opening. All of a sudden, you could see Jim coming up through the woods with his yellow Rokon, wearing his Six Days helmet. Ray thought, This is going to be good. Jim ripped through the group of riders waiting on the bottom and just gassed that Rokon. He got about two-thirds up the hill before he had to wiggle around a couple of downed riders. Once he got back on the throttle, the bike stood on its rear wheel. Ray says he can remember it clearly. "Jim looked like a big mountain man with both hands on the handlebars. As the bike was already past center, Jim pushed the bike up and off to the left side, keeping his momentum going up the hill. With the bike still running, Jim picked it up and gassed it, leaving everyone behind him. This all took place in less than two seconds. The riders still stuck and waiting at the bottom were just staring at each other in amazement." Ray added, "Jim was a bulldog on his bike. He was incredible. But when it came to Stan, he was a different rider. Stan was a smooth, gifted rider, easy on his bike."

Once Ed Schmidt was no longer racing ISDT qualifiers, he offered this same support to Ray. He would drive Ray to qualifiers, one of which was the Tennessee two-day qualifier. He was Ray's coach and mentor that whole weekend. He also took Ray to the Black Coal National Enduro. That year Ray was the overall B-Class winner on his Husqvarna automatic.

Ray recalled, "Ed didn't talk a lot, but when he did, you listened. He had the experience, and everything he said was valuable."

Ray wasn't the only local teenager who was inspired by Jim. Ed Schmidt had two sons, Ed Jr. and Patrick. They also looked up to Jim as a role model. He was intimidating and tough as nails. Ed Jr. remembers when he was around thirteen and attending the Potosi two-day qualifier—it was the last event of the day, the motocross test. Jim was on his factory Rokon. He got the holeshot and was just manhandling that Rokon around the track. He was winning the final moto when, all of a sudden, he pulled up next to the fence, yelling, "I need a screwdriver! My throttle came loose." Ed Jr. was standing there staring at Jim with his throttle cable wrapped around his handlebars. Ed Jr. didn't know what to do, since you could not assist a rider during a test. Somehow Jim mangaged to fix his throttle and took off. Ed Jr. did not know how Jim finished that day but stood there simply amazed at how Jim was basically riding that Rokon with one hand while holding the throttle steady with the other. Ed Jr. told me that Ed Sr. really respected Jim and Stan.

Ed Jr. experienced a lot of stuff growing up in St. Louis, as well as near the Husqvarna warehouse in Nashville, Tennessee. Dick Burelson and a few other ISDT riders worked and lived by the Nashville warehouse, too. There was an empty warehouse next to the Husqvarna warehouse where they would set up cones and flat track the leftover 125 Husqvarnas. Back in Missouri, Ed Jr. had the joys of meeting and hearing stories from Malcolm Smith, who would visit and ride on the #9 hill in Flat River. Ed Jr. also remembers seeing Steve McQueen riding at a local enduro.

From left to right: Jack Penton, Tom Clark, Dane Leimbach, Paul Danik, Doug Wilford, Jim Hollander, Jeff Penton, and Billy Uhl. Photo from the Mungenast Collection

Hagerty History

*I*t was at the Mungenast Museum gathering that I initially started talking to Stan about his ISDT history. I read he'd raced a Yamaha at the 1976 ISDT in Austria, and he also competed on one during the qualifiers. Stan and Jim were also chosen to be on the Yamaha two-day qualifier team in 1978 with the help of Kevin Hagerty. At this point, I found out that Kevin was the son of Pat Hagerty Sr., the same guy who managed the Doe Run Cycle Park for Dave Mungenast. What a small world; the name Kevin Hagerty didn't sound familiar to me at the time, but we would soon cross paths.

It occurred during the St. Louis Supercross activities. I was set up at the St. Louis Moto Museum selling my newly published book, *Finding #49 and America's Forgotten Motocross Team*, when a guy named Kevin Hagerty came up and said that he was friends with Rex Staten. I had the #49 Harley-Davidson MX team bike set up right behind me, so he got a picture with the bike to share with Rex. The more we talked, I could tell this guy was connected with the racing world, but it did not dawn on me that he was the Kevin Hagerty that Stan had mentioned. The next day at Supercross, I ran into him again at the "Legends and Heroes" display. That's when I found out he was originally from Missouri. Still, at that point, I didn't link Kevin to Stan and Jim. This wouldn't happen until the following month when Jim, Stan, and I attended Donelson Cycles' racer party. While there, we ran into Pat Hagerty, where I found out that Kevin was his brother and Stan reminded me of the connection. What a small world this was turning out to be. At this point, Kevin and I were friends on Facebook, so I immediately messaged him to let him know what I finally put together. And then I told him that I'd love to sit and talk about his time in the industry and his involvement with helping Stan and Jim get a Yamaha ride in 1978.

When I finally got the chance to sit down and talk with Kevin, I was not prepared for the stories I was about to hear. Here are just a few.

To start, in his early childhood, Kevin lived in my hometown of Ste. Genevieve, Missouri. I knew I'd felt connected to this guy beyond just our love of motorcycles. Kevin's history in off-road racing spans over forty years. Kevin started riding at nine years old. After his family moved north to Kirkwood, Missouri, his dad bought a Yamaha from Carl Donelson of Donelson Cycles in the early 1960s. He shared the bike with his brother, Pat. He started riding at the Pacific Cycle Playground before joining the army and going to Vietnam. Kevin first met Jim and Stan in the late 1960s at #9 hill, before it became St. Joe State Park. While away in Vietnam, his brother, Pat Hagerty, along with Jerry Radeackar, Rick Oxton, George

(Left to right) Local racers Jerry Radeackar, Max Lindemann, Pat Hagerty, and George Walker. March 1970, Centralia, IL. Photo by Kevin Hagerty

Walker, the Kohout brothers, Lloyd Stallman, and a few other guys, became the originators of motocross in the St. Louis area. Jay Clark, an up-and-coming local pro, learned from watching Pat Hagerty and Stallman. Jay said, "They were the hot shoes of the area when motocross first began in St. Louis—back when rubber band starts were the norm, and you waited for the gun with your clutch hand on your helmet. Back then, guys rode Bridgestone motorcycles with total loss ignition systems. If it ran, they raced it."

Kevin's family was really involved with the motocross scene. Kevin's dad, Pat Hagerty Sr., operated the Doe Run Cycle Park when he went to work for Dave Mungenast. The park was way ahead of its time. Lars Larsson, Malcolm Smith, Dick Burleson and many more legends all rode at the park. Kevin's other brother Terry showed them the ropes there. Honda and Yamaha used this area extensively for testing for three reasons: the difficult terrain, its off-the-beaten-path location, and because it had dealership support. When he returned from Vietnam in 1969, his brother Pat worked for Dave Mungenast at St. Louis Honda and was riding a Penton 125. It's been said that he was the first guy west of the Mississippi River that John Penton gave a bike to for the purpose of racing. He would race at Riverdale Speedway in St. Louis, where Carl Donelson would host 24-hour endurance flat-track and motocross races.

Kevin returned from Vietnam and started riding a Husky 360, and he had nothing but trouble with it. He tried to get a job at St. Louis Honda, but Dave quickly learned that Kevin didn't know squat about motorcycles. Kevin would then pursue a job with First Capitol Yamaha in St. Charles, Missouri, assembling motorcycles for owner Pat Seaman. From there, he learned about motorcycles and rose through the ranks. Ron Surdyke had the Kirkwood, Missouri, Yamaha dealership called Surdyke Cycles Inc., and Kevin took a job there as his service manager. Ron and Kevin's dad, Pat Sr., developed a MX track in St. Peters, Missouri that would become known as Cycle World USA. One thing led to another, and Ron's brother, Gary Surdyke, started his own Yamaha franchise in Festus, Missouri. Kevin would join Gary, becoming his first employee. No sooner did the Festus location open up on Bailey Road, than they got flooded out within ninety days from the rising Mississippi River. Thankfully, FEMA money helped them survive the disaster. When Kevin worked for Gary, he became a full-fledged Yamaha guy.

In 1972, Kevin broke his leg in a night motocross race at the St. Francis county fairgrounds. He was hit in the first corner during the second moto, and it almost ripped his leg off. He spent

St. Clair MX track. Clutch hand on the helmet start. Photo by Kevin Hagerty

(Previous) Terry Hagerty, Dick Mann, and Tim Hagerty at Doe Run Cycle Park. Photo from the Mungenast Collection
(Above) Kevin Hagerty's 1973 Bates ISDT support hat. Photo by Keith Geisner

the next thirteen months in a cast and three more on crutches. At that time, Gary Surdyke Yamaha in Festus was taking off with Gary and Kevin, both racing off-road. Kevin worked the 1973 ISDT as a support rider for Gary Surdyke. Because of that, he received a Bates hat for registered support people. No racers got a hat, just the support people. Kevin said Gary almost didn't finish in 1973. "Had we not swapped out a whole rear brake assembly on the bike, he never would've finished." He added, "The unspoken rule of the ISDT was anything you can get away with was fair." One time, he saw six Czechs in a bike compound gathered around a bike. Within ten minutes, they pulled off a shock, rebuilt it, and stuck it back on—with parts they had stashed in their pockets. If you didn't see it, it didn't happen.

Around 1973, Kevin took a job with Yamaha, the parent company. Yamaha started a service team, and they needed service technicians. The national service manager got Kevin's name from the district sales guy (and Gary also promoted Kevin to Yamaha). Off goes Kevin to work with Yamaha in Cudahy, Wisconsin. Yamaha had a parts distribution center there, and that's where they held their training classes for mechanics. Kevin was a road tech and regional service representative for Carl Donelson and all the surrounding states. He did that for a year—until, one day, Kevin's curiosity would lead him to his next journey with Yamaha.

Kevin was an off-road enduro guy. At the Yamaha training center in Wisconsin, they had several bikes around at all times for classroom training and to test ride around the facility. One day, Kevin took a 1975 Yamaha MX250 and was determined to set it up like an enduro bike. He first tore the motor down and replaced the left side crank with a left side crank from a Yamaha DT model, so he could mount an external flywheel and lighting coil to run lights. This was followed by a headlight and taillight from a Yamaha TY trials bike, some sprocket size changes for the proper gearing, and a modified chain tensioner. Kevin would ride the bike at the local motorcycle enduros in the upper Midwest.

During this time, a group of Yamaha engineers from Japan would stop in and tour the facility. This happened about once a month. Except for this time, one of them took notice of Kevin's modified MX250. He stopped dead in his tracks and asked, "Who did this to this motorcycle?" Kevin's boss threw him under the bus. The engineer started asking Kevin all about the bike: How was he powering the light? How did he mount the chain tensioner off a TY? How did the flywheel affect the powerband? He soon was test riding and demonstrating the bike. The engineer, Jim Koike, was very impressed with Kevin's demonstration. Within two weeks Kevin's boss informed him he was moving to California to work in the new test department, led by Jim Koike, working with the soon-to-be-released Yamaha IT series bikes. Kevin's wife was pregnant at the time. They moved to Los Angeles in late 1975. Kevin started in January 1976 and was basically paid to play and ride motorcycles for testing purposes all day, riding at Saddleback Park, Indian Dunes, Carlsbad, Escape Country, Corona Raceway, and several other local venues.

When the IT250 preproduction bikes came out, Kevin and John Fero spent two-and-a-half seasons on the National Enduro circuit. John rode, and Kevin supported him. From 1977 through 1979, Kevin was heavily involved with Yamaha's ISDT teams. In 1978 at the ISDT in Sweden, the pits were on an old airplane landing strip, and the walk was long to gas up. Kevin strapped on roller skates to speed up the transport of fuel between fill-ups, leaving the competing pit crews in his dust. Kevin was manager of the 1979 Yamaha ISDT team and remembered it as the biggest Yamaha team to compete in the ISDT.

In 1978, Yamaha started an ISDT two-day qualifier team. Kevin was able to help Stan and Jim get on the team and receive Yamaha IT support bikes. Kevin dropped their names and their racing record; the rest is history.

Stan remembered this funny story about Kevin. It was during the two-day qualifier in Rose City, Michigan, in 1978. Kevin was gaining a reputation, like Bob Hannah, on racing rental cars on motocross and enduro courses. Kevin was using his rented station wagon to carry the fuel to all the stops along the route. I'm sure it was smooth driving. Needless to say, by the end of the day, the spare tire compartment was filled to the top with gas. Kevin couldn't return it like this. So, using a hammer and a screwdriver, he produced a drain at the bottom of the spare tire compartment relieving it of all the gas—problem solved.

Ron Ribolzi was also a support rider for Yamaha. John, Kevin, and Ron signed up as a

FERO, RIBOLZI GANG UP ON

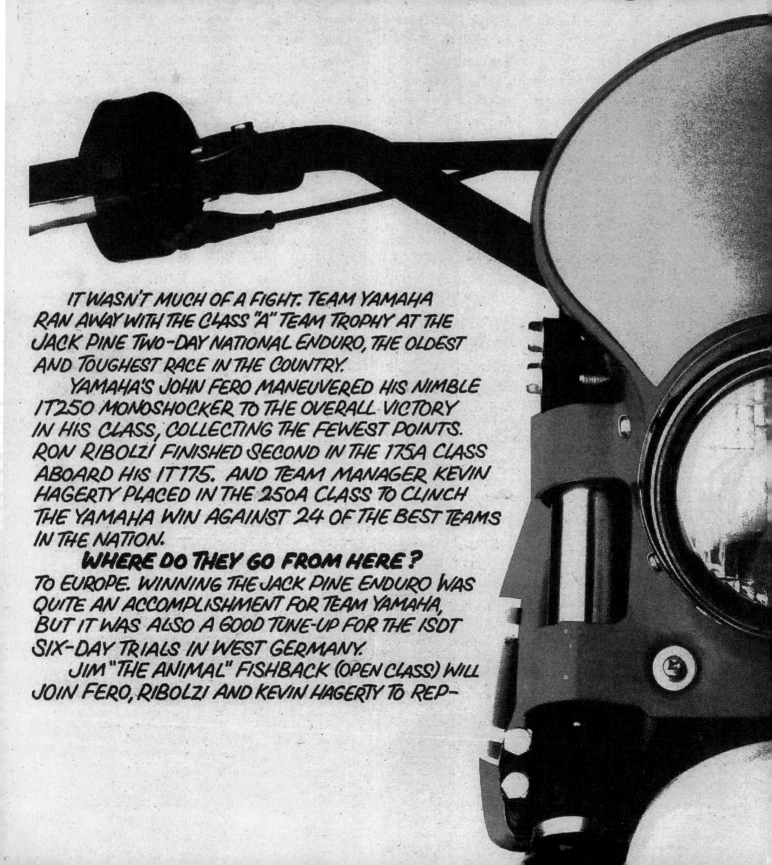

IT WASN'T MUCH OF A FIGHT. TEAM YAMAHA RAN AWAY WITH THE CLASS "A" TEAM TROPHY AT THE JACK PINE TWO-DAY NATIONAL ENDURO, THE OLDEST AND TOUGHEST RACE IN THE COUNTRY.

YAMAHA'S JOHN FERO MANEUVERED HIS NIMBLE IT250 MONOSHOCKER TO THE OVERALL VICTORY IN HIS CLASS, COLLECTING THE FEWEST POINTS. RON RIBOLZI FINISHED SECOND IN THE 175A CLASS ABOARD HIS IT175. AND TEAM MANAGER KEVIN HAGERTY PLACED IN THE 250A CLASS TO CLINCH THE YAMAHA WIN AGAINST 24 OF THE BEST TEAMS IN THE NATION.

WHERE DO THEY GO FROM HERE?

TO EUROPE. WINNING THE JACK PINE ENDURO WAS QUITE AN ACCOMPLISHMENT FOR TEAM YAMAHA, BUT IT WAS ALSO A GOOD TUNE-UP FOR THE ISDT SIX-DAY TRIALS IN WEST GERMANY.

JIM "THE ANIMAL" FISHBACK (OPEN CLASS) WILL JOIN FERO, RIBOLZI AND KEVIN HAGERTY TO REP-

AND HAGERTY
OLD JACK PINE.

RESENT YAMAHA (AND THE UNITED STATES) IN THE GRUELING COMPETITION. FERO, RIBOLZI, AND FISHBACK HAVE ALREADY TAKEN ELEVEN GOLD MEDALS AND ONE SILVER IN 13 AMA-QUALIFYING STARTS THIS YEAR.

HOW TO CONQUER EUROPE IN YOUR SPARE TIME.
RACING IS ONLY A PART-TIME ACTIVITY FOR HAGERTY AND FERO. THEY WORK FULL-TIME FOR THE YAMAHA ENGINEERING DEPARTMENT.

SO YOU CAN BE DARN SURE THAT EVERYTHING TEAM YAMAHA LEARNS ABOUT TRIALS COMPETITION IS USED TO MAKE OUR IT MONOSHOCKERS EVEN BETTER.

AT YAMAHA, WE BELIEVE THE BEST WAY TO MAKE WINNING MOTORCYCLES IS TO LET WINNERS MAKE THEM.

YAMAHA
When you know how they're built.

team for the 1979 Jack Pine 500 two-day endurance event, and they won. The win was a double-edged sword, though. It was fine for Ron and John to win, but Yamaha wasn't happy with Kevin. Kevin was a tester, not a racer. The Japanese were strict about what roles they hired you to play. They won the manufacturing team award for that race, as well. Kevin still has the cowbell trophy, and that race was Kevin's claim to fame. And he didn't lose his job, so it ended up being a win-win.

Kevin said Chris Carter was a test rider before there were test riders for the pre-production prototype IT bikes. He said one time he came with Chris Carter, Mark Porter, and Bill Stewart to Missouri with bikes for testing. They were headquartered at the Potosi Lions Club and did testing for a few days. Carter worked through Bill Stewart, which was through the racing department, kind of like a contract racer. Meanwhile, John Fero and Kevin were "the testing department." Even though John was super competitive, Yamaha told him where, when, and how to race, which was "with more control," because they were testing. Whereas Chris Carter was working for the race department. Chris and Bill Stewart worked for race team manager Pete Schick. Pete was more focused on the Yamaha road racing team and on Kenny Roberts. According to Kevin, Pete would just throw Chris and Bill money to stay out of his hair. Not until Kenny Clark came around did the off-road racing get serious. Kenny hired Broc Glover, Bob Hannah, and Rex Staten.

Kevin got to test ride with Bob Hannah out at Saddleback Park. Kevin said that people who make money in the sport today have Bob Hannah to thank. He was the best rider Kevin had ever seen. Bob came at every race with the attitude that he was going to win, and that was the only thing that mattered. Bob had the will to win. Bob Hannah's dominance in every class he entered in 1977 made the AMA create the "Bob Hannah" rule. The AMA feared a Hannah sweep of every Championship, so they stopped holding single class Nationals, choosing to combine them on the same day. In 1978, Bob won twenty-two straight motos on practically a stock bike. After his twenty-second win, they gave the bike away to a lucky spectator.

Kevin spent forty-five years in California. In the late 1980s, he started an insurance agency that his daughter currently runs in Hunting Beach. In 2006, he decided to get back in the business, to give back, so he got involved with the motorcycle tour company Alaska Rider Tours, owned by Phil Freeman. Kevin helped Phil expand the business and the name changed to MotoQuest. MotoQuest covers twenty-three countries and has over 100 motorcycles in its fleet. They currently employ sixteen people.

(Previous) Fero, Ribolzi, and Hagerty take the Jack Pine. Photo Provided by Cycle News

The Preservation Begins

Now that the majority of work was finished on the Harley-Davidson MX team bike, I decided to focus my attention on Jim's Husqvarna—to try to have it preserved within a year of discovering it. It helps to set goals, so I had roughly six months to finish Jim's bike. I placed his bike up on my motorcycle lift and started to take it apart carefully. My goal was to disassemble the entire bike, clean it up, replace any bearings and seals that were worn out, but preserve all of the original paint and inspection marks that were placed on the bike. As the parts came off, I'd make note of anything that caught my attention.

Everything came off easily and, as each part was removed, I placed it on the floor. Once it was down to the bare frame, I was ready to take a picture of the entire bike in pieces on the floor to kick off my preservation. Then, I was going to go in reverse: place the frame back on the stand and start cleaning it, taking great care not to remove any original paint and inspection marks. Part by part, I would do this over the next few months. The forks and the Curnutt rear shocks were cleaned and rebuilt with new seals and oil. As I was cleaning the parts of the bike, I kept in mind that during inspection at the ISDT, they would scribe the rider's number into the inspection paint of the parts. I noted this, seeing the number 319 scribed in several areas on the bike. The number 319 was Jim's number at the 1976 Austria ISDT. For the most part, the bike was in decent shape. All the major pieces were there, except the number plates, or so I thought.

As I got closer to getting the bike back together, I started thinking about the parts I didn't have. I'd recently seen photos of Jim in Austria. They were shared by Gary Surdyke and a few Facebook friends on the Leroy Winters Memorial ISDT Reunion Ride group. From the pics, I could tell the obvious parts that were missing were the number plates, front headlight, and the airbox lid had been swapped out. Luckily, the Preston Petty number plates that were used on Jim's bike were still available today, and the correct airbox lid was easily sourced on eBay.

One day when I was cleaning up the exhaust and motor, I sent Stan Rubottom some progress photos. He commented that I was doing a great job. When I asked if he knew of anyone who may have pictures of Jim while he was in Austria, he mentioned some mutual friends of theirs by the names of Tony Budde, Wayne Gibson, and Tim Hamilton. As luck would have it, the following day, Tony and Wayne paid Stan a visit, and they brought their photo albums. Stan texted me some awesome photos of Jim while he was in Austria. The pictures were so crisp that I noticed additional items on his bike while in Austria—the parts I was missing: license plate, taillight, supply bag on the rear fender, tank bag, gold throttle grip, speedo, speedo cable, cable drive, and a brake switch. All these new findings added to the work and research I needed to do.

Jim Simmons' 1976 ISDT Husqvarna ready for cleanup. Photo by Keith Geisner

Rear Fender Items

*F*inding answers to the missing parts was exciting and enlightening. For example, what I thought was a tool bag on the rear fender was actually an inner tube, miscellaneous tools and parts wrapped up in a plastic bag to keep them dry, secured by rubber bands that were made from a red Barum brand inner tube cut into strips. Next to the bag was a light, but no Husqvarna taillight. I called Jim to see what he used for a taillight. He said he believed it was a marker/clearance lamp he'd purchased from a local hardware store. Sourcing the exact taillight was challenging, so I found the closest thing I could. Mimicking the inner tube bag was simple. The red rubber strapping was sourced off eBay to resemble the inner tube bands Jim used. I had found some of the old red bands Jim used in his toolbox, but they were too far deteriorated to be of help. It wasn't until a couple of years later, when an exact Barum inner tube was found and duplicate bands were produced, that I was able to replicate that part exactly.

Also, on the rear fender of Jim's bike in Austria was a license plate. But there were no clear pictures of this license plate that I could see and copy. So, instead, I made my own plate, one that commemorated Jim and his accomplishments in Austria that year. I did not want to add any more holes in the rear fender, so I used the existing license plate holes to mount the custom plate. To mount the taillight and inner tube bag to the rear fender, I made a bracket that I mounted into the existing holes in the rear fender and then mounted these items to the bracket. The result turned out pretty good. It wasn't until Wayne Gibson uncovered an additional photo showing a good image of Jim's license plate used in Austria that I could make a similar duplicate plate.

Extra details found in Wayne Gibson's photo: Screw driver in steering stem, license plate markings, tank bag, gold medal grip, and fender bag. Photo by Wayne Gibson

The Motor

*T*he motor just needed a good cleaning from sitting all those years with dirt and oil on it. It also had an inspection paint smudge with his riding number scribed in it, and I wanted to be careful not to remove that. I checked compression before removing it from the frame, and it checked within spec. It also shifted well and had great spark, so I was not going to worry about a complete teardown and rebuild—just clean it up. One thing of note on the motor were the holes in the lower fin of the head and upper fin of the cylinder. Those were in line with each other. These holes were used for the wire inspection seal to keep riders from tampering with their top ends throughout the six days. Seeing this told me it still had the same head and cylinder on it used in Austria. The extra parts that came with the bike had a few used pistons and a rod. That told me that after Austria, the motor was rebuilt, which makes sense since I'd found out it seized a few times during Six Days. More on that later.

Frame and motor cleaned and coming together. Photo by Keith Geisner

Tank bag found. Photo by Keith Geisner

Tank Bag

*T*he tank bag was hard to find. I saw a couple of examples on the internet, and I believe there's one on display at the Mungenast Museum. What stood out about this bag was the leather flap, which was de-bossed with a logo. I finally got the correct identification from Ed Schmidt's son Pat who said the tank bag was sold by Husqvarna. I wanted to do the bag right, so I decided that until I find the same type of tank bag, the bike will go without it. Fast forward to 2020 and—thanks to a lead from Ray Mungenast—I found a matching Husqvarna tank bag for Jim's bike.

Throttle Grip

When I received Jim's bike in October of 2017, one thing I noticed was the throttle grip was too far gone to identify. It was black and deteriorated badly. I could make out one word on it: gold. The left-hand grip was just fine and reusable, but a different brand. This just didn't make sense to me. Not until I saw the photos from Tony Budde could I put it all together. Tony

Gold Medal brand throttle grip found in Jim's toolbox. Photo by Keith Geisner

had a picture of Jim's bike. The throttle grip was a gold color, and the left-hand grip was black, like what was currently on it. I thought at first, it was an error in the negative, but then Tony had a photo of Dick Burleson, Malcolm Smith, and Ken Maahs all together—and I noticed on Malcolm's bike that he also was running a gold grip on the throttle and a black grip on the left-hand. I found this interesting and hit the internet to find one of these gold grips. I found out that it was a Malcolm Smith Gold Medal brand grip. That was the good news. The bad news was it seemed unlikely I'd ever find another one. I pulled out Jim's toolbox to see what parts were in it. Maybe I could find some clues. And there it was: a usable Malcolm Smith Gold Medal grip on a spare throttle tube sitting in the toolbox. What a lucky break. Jim's bike even had the solid aluminum "J" bars that Malcolm Smith distributed.

The routing of Jim's throttle cable was like nothing I had ever seen; instead of going in front of the handlebars and between the forks and frame to the carb, it was routed straight toward the rider, down to the right-side front gas tank mount, and then to the carb. This throttle cable routing was also noted on photos I saw of Ed Schmidt's 1973 ISDT #284 Husqvarna.

Dick Burleson, Malcolm Smith, and Ken Maahs in Austria 1976. Notice Malcolm's Gold Medal throttle grip. Photo by Tony Budde

Number Plates

*T*ony Budde and Wayne Gibson's photos also provided some great images of Jim's number plates when he raced in Austria. Preston Petty Products number plates are still available today, thanks to Paul Stannard. So, it was a no-brainer to order new side panels and a new headlight. The tricky part was matching the number font. In the 1976 ISDT, the numbers were painted on with black spray bomb using stencils. I saw this in an online video about the 1976 ISDT. I researched and found a similar military number font on the internet, made my own stencils, and applied the numbers the same way. After several attempts, I finally found a style and size font for the numbers that made me happy. I would send photos to Stan every time I tried a new number font until I had it just right. I hope I didn't bug him too much. He reminded me that only I would notice any imperfections. This really took the bike back to the same appearance as depicted in Tony and Wayne's photos.

Numbers were applied by the same method used at the 1976 ISDT in Austria. Photo by Keith Geisner.

Speedo and brake switch spotted. Photo by Wayne Gibson

Speedo and Brake Switch

Tony and Wayne's photos told a story. You could see things on Jim's bike in photos that were taken earlier—at the beginning of the Austria ISDT—that would not be on Jim's bike by the end of the Austria ISDT. Those items were a speedo and brake light switch. Jim could not remember why he would have needed a speedo for the Austria race or why a brake light switch was needed, but you can see these items in the photos that Tony took. My only guess was that these items were needed to make them legal to ride around Austria until the actual race started. But Jim and Stan couldn't remember any details about either of these items from the Austria race. I would later find out that, at the time, the rule book for the ISDT stated that to be street legal, the bikes had to have a speedo mounted in eyesight and in working order. During tech inspection, however, they were rarely checked for function. After inspections, they were never checked again, so usually there was a pile of speedos in the work area the morning of day one.

Wheels

Rear Sun rim date code 01 77. Photo by Keith Geisner

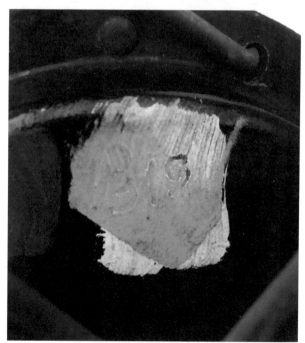

Example of paint dabs and bike number scribed on the front hub. Photo by Keith Geisner

Another item that puzzled me was the rear rim. Jim ran aftermarket Sun rims on his Husqvarna. The tires were still the original ones he ran during that timeframe. I could tell because the date code on them confirmed they were made in 1976. Same with the rims, but I did find one issue: Sun rims were stamped with a manufacturing date as Jim's front wheel was dated 1976 but his rear rim was dated 1977, which places it after the 1976 ISDT in Austria. Another conflicting piece of the puzzle was that the tube stem location paint on the rear wheel was green. But, in Tony Budde's photos, it was red. Sometime after the ISDT in Austria, the rear wheel was replaced. This bike may have more races on it than I'd thought, and that may explain all the extra parts that came with it. More on these findings later. One last note: the front hub wasn't a stock 1976 WR hub, but a 1975 CR model conical hub. Remember, this bike was built from parts picked by Ed Schmidt.

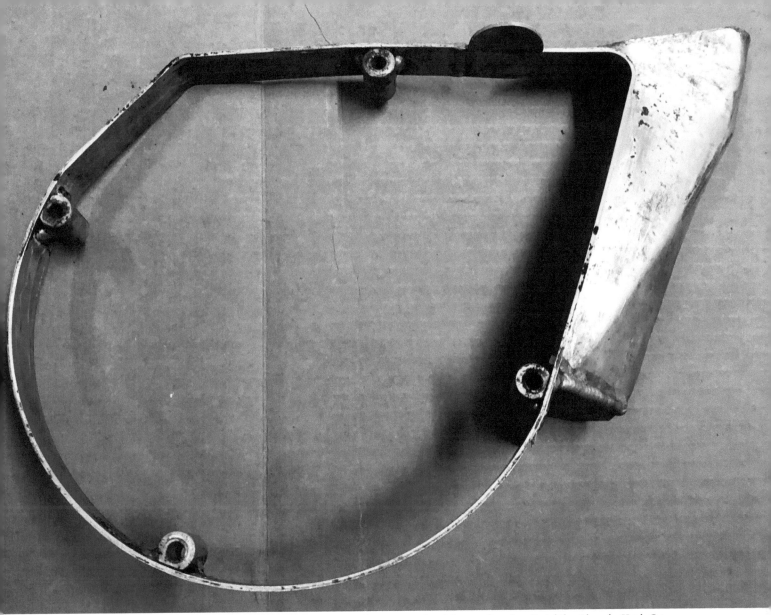

Aluminum airbox lid spacer found on Jim's bike. Photo by Keith Geisner

Airbox

There was something about the airbox that caught my attention as well. It looked like a one-inch aluminum extension was added between the cover and body to allow for a bigger air filter element to be installed. Also, the lid wasn't the correct one based on Tony and Wayne's photos. When I received Jim's bike, it had an airbox cover with the 1974 World Champion H. Mikkola decal on it for the 1975 models. The airbox lid that Jim would have used in Austria was smooth, with no raised square frame for the displacement number, and the words "cross country" were displayed along the top. I found one on eBay, along with an American flag decal.

(Left and middle) Scribing on Mikuni carburetor. (Right) Old duct tape hanging onto the rear frame section. Photos by Keith Geisner

Carburetor

The 1976 Husqvarnas came from the factory with a Bing carburetor, but not Jim's. His bike, along with the other ISDT Husqvarnas in 1976, were fitted with Mikuni carburetors. The body of the carb and bowl had 38mm scribed on them, but the bowl also had R&D scribed on it. Did that stand for research and development?

Misc. Items

I noticed traces of old duct tape on the front down tube of the frame and on the left-hand side of the frame by the rear fender. After looking at Tony and Wayne's photos, I could see that duct tape was holding Jim's ignition wiring harness to the front down tube and the rear taillight harness. Stan said there was duct tape everywhere when working at Brown Carpet, so they used it anywhere they could. Another item of note was Jim's spark plug cap—it was an aftermarket Malcolm Smith brand, as well. Oh, and by the way, that extra exhaust pipe I got from Johnny Waller was the same pipe Jim used in Austria. The exhaust that was mounted on the bike was added later and would help shed light on the misdated rear rim.

Riding Buddies

I would eventually reach out to Tony Budde to scan the photos he took at the 1976 ISDT when he and Wayne Gibson went to watch Jim and Stan compete. Tony met Wayne Gibson when he started working at Chrysler in Fenton, Missouri, in 1973. Tony said Wayne was racing a 250 Yamaha motocross bike and, through him, he met Jim and Stan and a lot of their friends who rode enduros and lived in the Lead Belt area. Up to that point, Tony did a lot of riding himself. He said, "In July of 1970, I bought my first bike from Donelson's store on the corner of Morganford and Delor across from the Bevo Mill. It was a 1970 Yamaha 125 Enduro that cost five hundred dollars. At this time, everybody was graduating to real dirt bikes and the street bikes disappeared. We mostly rode in poker runs at Ebo on Highway 8. No time involved, just racing each other. There were a lot of motocross tracks popping up and a lot of guys raced at them. Motorcycle clubs were forming in every town and they started having enduros on Sundays, so we started riding in them. The fast riders were riding big bore bikes in the open class. My second bike was a 250 Ossa Pioneer. I was going to buy a 250 Yamaha Enduro, but the Ossa had a 21-inch front wheel, aluminum wheels, and knobby tires for nine hundred dollars. It was more suited for enduros than the street and trail Yamaha." With Tony's photos scanned, I contacted Wayne to see what photos he had of the event.

I took this time to reach out to Wayne Gibson, as well, since he took a lot of photos while vacationing in Austria. He did not disappoint. Wayne's history with motorcycles is as follows: "I started riding dirt bikes in 1969. At the time, we were boating and camping almost every weekend at Lake Wappapello, and a lot of people had small dirt bikes to ride around the campgrounds. I bought a new Yamaha 90 Enduro but only kept it for a short time. I went trail riding with some friends who had 250s and saw right away that the 90 wasn't big enough. I traded it for a 250 DT1 Yamaha and was hooked from then on."

"I started competing in enduros shortly thereafter. The first one I ever entered was near Potosi, and the guys I went with agreed to ride together and help one another. I saw right away that that was not the proper way to compete so, the next race, I said it was everyone for themselves. I think I got third place in the second one. I rode two or three DT1s, then a 250 YZ, and the last one was a 450WR Husky that I bought from Jim Simmons. It was like new when I bought it."

"I knew Jim and Stan when we were doing all the camping and boating in the late 1960s. They were both great barefoot skiers. One story I can tell you is that Jim had a tunnel hull boat with a 125 hp Mercury on it. He got it trimmed up too high one day and the wind caught under it and crashed. It tore it up, and I think it punctured Jim's eardrum. I have tons of great memories of Jim and Stan. We went coast to coast to a lot of races—California, Massachusetts, Texas, Ohio, Indiana, Kansas, Michigan, Illinois, Alabama, and many more. These two guys will always be at the top of my list of great friends."

"I was never in the same class of Jim and Stan, not even close, but I was a decent competitor. I guess the highlight of my racing was in a national enduro at Potosi in 1972. I was riding that YZ250 and won the 250B-Class and the overall B-Class. The worst thing that ever happened to me was when we all went to Michigan and ran the Jack Pine National. I hit a guy head-on who was coming backward on the trail. It broke my wrist, my kneecap, and my collarbone. I was in the hospital for about a week and then had to fly home."

"As far as growing up in this area, it couldn't have been much better. St. Joe Lead Company owned most of the land around here, and we had plenty of places to hunt, fish, and ride dirt bikes. Many times, we would start out on a Saturday morning and ride all day, seldom riding the same trails twice."

Both Tony and Wayne would share photos with me of the Austria ISDT that had never

Jim fixing a rear flat on his Husqvarna during the 1976 ISDT in Austria. Note his hip pack now in Tim Hamilton's collection. Photo by Tony Budde

been seen until now. The photos helped considerably in the preservation of Jim's bike.

The other name Stan mentioned was Tim Hamilton. I got Tim's number from Tony. When I reached out to Tim, he told me he was also friends with Dennis and Craz. He first met them at the 2006 ISDT Reunion Ride at St. Joe State Park. Craz was riding an Ossa motorcycle and it caught Tim's eye because he had that same bike back in 1969. This started a motorcycle friendship and they would always see each other at the vintage motorcycle events. Prior to Johnny Waller purchasing Jim's Husqvarna, Tim had an opportunity to buy it. He was helping Craz downsize his collection and ended up with all the trophies that Craz had received from Jim Simmons. He also received the tool bag hip pack that Jim wore at the Austria ISDT. It was a real treat to look through Jim's old trophies and see the items he had on him during the Six Days. Throughout the years, Tim would donate some of Jim's bigger trophies to some of the motorcycle museums in St. Louis.

Jim's USA ISDT helmet wearing the visor he used on his 1978 Mexico ISDT helmet. Photo by Keith Geisner

• • •

*I*n the process of trying to restore Jim's bike to 100 percent accuracy, I reached out to Stan and asked if he had a speedo, speedo mount, and watch holder. He said he did have some of these items, and he invited me down to check them out and to see if I wanted to add them to the bike. I planned a day off work and went down to visit. Jim said he had a few more things to give me, so I visited him first. The one-year date was quickly approaching since I'd first brought Jim's bike home, and my goal was to have it finished. I had two weeks to go.

During our first visit, he gave me his 1978 Mexico ISDT helmet. It was missing its visor and, since receiving it, I've been looking for one with no such luck. You can see this visor in the Mexico team picture with Lars Larsson and Fred Cameron. I was surprised that, on my second visit, Jim handed me his USA ISDT helmet. To my delight, his Mexico visor was on it. He said the helmet was one of three he had received while riding for the USA, and he added that his two daughters, April and Krista, had his other ones. Now all I had to do was find a black visor like the one he used in 1976. I asked him why they used duct tape on their visors where it attached to the helmet. "Does it keep out water?" I asked. Jim said, "They used duct tape because sometimes the snaps would fail and the visor would come loose."

He also gave me his three prized trophies, which were his Jack Pine, Burr Oak, and

Stan and Jim with their 1972 Berkshire Club trophy.
Photo by Keith Geisner

Stan Rubottom with his 1975 and 1976 ISDT USA helmets.
Photo by Keith Geisner

Berkshire Club trophies. He shared his 1973 ISDT USA suit bag, too. The riders were given matching suits and suit bags when they were representing the USA in the 1973 ISDT in Dalton, Massachusetts. All these items meant a lot, not only because they are a part of ISDT history, but because Jim trusted me to be their caretaker. He also shared a newspaper clipping that he and his wife had found since my last visit. It was an article from *The Daily Journal* that featured a photo of Jim standing next to his trophies. The article talked about him coming out of retirement to compete in the 1983 Flat River Grand Prix at St. Joe Park. I only had one page of the two-page story. More on that second page later.

After we finished going through Jim's items, it was time to meet up with Stan Rubottom, who lived just down the road. I grabbed the Club trophy and put it in the truck. When we made it to Stan's house, I had Jim and Stan hold the trophy so I could take a picture. The only team member missing was James Hollander. We followed Stan into his garage and he showed us his current bike—a 2017 KTM, with maintenance records and suspension settings clearly noted on the handlebars. He had a nice setup: a full-size cargo Ford van loaded with all his gear and tools, ready to go at a moment's notice.

Stan pulled a box off the shelf next to two USA ISDT helmets (1975–1976). I had him pose for a picture with his helmets. Inside the box, he had a collection of ISDT memorabilia—a new pair of Malcolm Smith Gold Medal gloves given to him by Malcolm himself at the Austria 1976 ISDT, an Austria ISDT leather belt buckle, 1976 USA ISDT team gloves, numerous enduro patches, enduro programs, speedometers, and watch magnifiers. Each item came with a detailed story that only Stan could tell. Other items of note were his USA ISDT jacket that he'd worn in Austria in 1976, his 1975 USA ISDT team jacket, and his 1976 USA gear bag. Stan picked out a speedometer, a watch holder with a Torino train watch, along with Husqvarna bar mounts to donate to Jim's Husqvarna preservation. I was grateful to receive these items.

Since I had Jim and Stan both together, I took this time to ask some questions and fill in any missing stories that may have been forgotten over the last forty-plus years. One of those stories was about the famous chat dump you used to see while driving into Flat River, Missouri. It was a popular spot for kids to ride their motorcycles to the top and drink beer. The story goes that Jim, on his 125 Yamaha, could only make it halfway up the hill and then he would have to get off and carry his beer the rest of the way up. Well, Jim was getting tired of this, so one day he walked into Donelson Cycles in Flat River and asked what kinds of bikes they had that could get him up to the top of that chat dump. The salesman took him to the back, where he showed Jim a BSA 441 Victor. The salesman told him it may be a little tricky to start, but that it would do the job. The bike was able to get Jim to the top of the chat dump so he could join the rest of his friends. It even hauled the beer cooler up, too.

Jim and his daughter, April. Photo by Jim Simmons

I asked about another story I'd read in *Cycle News*. It was a letter to the editor by Michael A. DiPrete, the team manager of the factory Rokon team, it stated:

> I wrote to you on July 1, 1974, objection to an article about the length of time it takes to change tires on a Rokon, written by Mr. Ron Schneiders. In the article Mr. Schneiders told your many readers how it took 50 minutes to change the tire on a Rokon. Well, I have some factual news for Mr. Schneiders and your readers. On September 15, 1974, the Kaw Valley National Enduro was held in Kansas. In that event Jim Simmons, riding a RT340 Rokon automatic, took first place in the heavy weight class and fourth place overall. At the end of the event a tire change contest was held and guess who won – Jim Simmons changed the tire on a RT340 Rokon automatic in three minutes and forty-five seconds and won the tire changing event.[11]

After hearing about the article, both Jim and Stan laughed. Jim said they were giving away a pair of new High Point boots to the winner of the tire changing competition, and he told everyone he wasn't even going to take boots to the event because he knew he was going to win. His daughter April went along for the ride, and he told her when he gave her the sign, to roll his

Gary Surdyke's bike being hauled by Jim and Stan. Photo by Jim Simmons

new tire out to him. She delivered the tire on cue and Jim won his boots. Stan also noted that he rode up on Jim near the end of the race and caught him letting air out of his tires. By dropping the air pressure in Jim's tires, he was guaranteed to have the tire beads broken loose in time for the tire changing contest, adding to his speedy tire change and a Rokon tire change record.

Another funny story Jim told me was about their travels to the Berkshire two-day in 1972. Their friend and Yamaha dealership owner, Gary Surdyke, asked if he and Stan could haul his bike to the qualifier. Jim and Stan strapped it to the hitch hauler on their van. During one of their gas stops, they found a sign that read: Pure Junk.

They bought the sign and hung it on Gary's Yamaha. They took a picture as proof to show to Gary. Gary's bike was displayed the remainder of the trip for all to see. Both Jim and Stan couldn't stop chuckling as they told that story.

• • •

I was fortunate to be friends with Gary Surdyke on Facebook, so it was easy for me to reach out to him with questions of his ISDT past. I asked Gary when he first met Jim and Stan, and he said he noticed Stan and Jim in 1970. "Those two guys were always near or at the front of any event, along with Ed Schmidt and Dave Mungenast," he said.

Gary started riding when he and his brother Ron got Honda S-90s in 1965. They soon got bored with the street and found riding off-road was much more fun. Gary's first go at off-road racing didn't start out too well. He raced his first enduro in 1967 at the Steel Helmet in Cedar Hill, Missouri, on his S-90. He geared it down, added a high pipe and knobby tires. He accidently overfilled the crank case and it oil fouled the spark plug. He did not finish. Down the road, he would eventually win the Steel Helmet Enduro. He then replaced the Honda with a Bridgestone 175, which ended up being another mistake. It had a total loss ignition system, which meant once his battery was dead, so was he. He had to carry a second battery to be able to run all day, which he stored behind the number plate. At the 1967 Busted Piston Enduro in Potosi, Missouri, the hot wire from the battery came in contact with the throttle cable and started a fire. Needless to say, that was the end of the race for Gary. After the Bridgestone, he bought a 1967 BSA Victor. The first event he entered with the BSA, the tranny busted. The second event he entered, the oil line came loose and seized the crank. It wasn't until Yamaha came out with the DT-1 did good things start happening for Gary in off-road racing.

When I asked Gary what prompted him to start competing for the ISDT, he told me the movie *On Any Sunday* is what inspired him. After seeing the movie, he called Mike Vancil with the AMA and asked what it took to be selected. Mike told Gary that the first ISDT qualifier ever in the USA was being held in Oregon, called the Trask Mountain ISDT qualifier. He said go and compete and get a gold medal. Gary talked fellow competitor Ray Biesk from Illinois into competing as well. Gary also recruited Pat Hagerty Sr. to pit for them. He bought a new 1971 Ford Econoline van, and off they went. Both Ray and Gary won gold medals. They both met John Penton there, as well. Penton was one minute behind them and, after a long gravel road section, he taught Ray and Gary a little trail etiquette. Gary said they were riding Yamaha RT-1s and we were roosting too much gravel. Afterward, John straightened them out on this matter. That same year, Gary would go on to become the overall grand champion of the Busted Piston National Enduro in Potosi, Missouri.

Gary Surdyke at the 1973 ISDT. Photo by Kevin Hagerty

Gary ended up competing in a total of four ISDTs. The first being at the 1971 Isle of Man, where he won silver. The second, in 1972, was in Czechoslovakia, where he did not finish. Gary said Kevin Hagerty was his right-hand man, and he never forgot him running the shop in his absence with his blood-soaked cast. In 1973, in Dalton, Massachusetts, he won bronze. And finally, in 1975, he competed in the Isle of Man, where he did not finish again. At the Isle of Man in 1971, Gary said Rolf Tibblin, World MX Champion, was a big help for the USA effort. At the team meeting before the event, Rolf was planning pre-run routes. He said he had a key to all the gates on the island. Come to find out, his key was a big hammer to bust the locks.

Prototype Yamaha TT500 test ridden at Ringo Springs MX Park. Photo by Kevin Hagerty

In 1975, Gary did not officially qualify for the ISDT. Around August 1, he received a call from Al Eames, AMA ISDT manager, telling him they had one more slot available. Al knew Gary well enough to know he could put something together with short notice. Rumors were out that Yamaha was about to release the TT500, the first competitive four-stroke from Japan. Al told Gary to see if Yamaha would give him an early release of the TT500 for his ISDT ride. Gary called, and Yamaha made the deal. (On a side note, Yamaha had Gary testing prototype TT500s and IT400s earlier that year at the Ringo Springs track in Reynolds County, Missouri.) The TT500 drew much attention at the ISDT. On the third day, running on a gold medal pace, Gary stalled the bike on a climb and could not get it restarted. Finally, he realized the front brake perch slid and pinched the kill button, shorting it out. By the time he found the root cause, he had already houred out, putting him out of medal contention. Afterward, Gary sold the TT500 to Torsten Hallman, with Lars Larsson being the middleman. It was the first TT500 in Europe, and it became the first Bengt Åberg Yamaha four-stroke.

Gary Surdyke and his 1971 Yamaha, #211, raced at the Isle of Man ISDT. Photo by Keith Geisner

Gary would help Stan get his Yamaha support ride in 1976. Yamaha furnished Stan a Yamaha IT400 right before the New Jersey two-day qualifier where he won a gold medal. After qualifying for the 1976 ISDT, Stan was invited to test ride next year's Yamaha IT400 models at Surdyke's Ringo Springs MX Park. Stan would go onto to race that same pre-production bike in the 1976 ISDT.

Qualifying

In 1973, Jim and Stan embarked on their professional off-road racing careers when they were selected to be members of the first ever Rokon factory racing team. Stan could remember it clearly when they met with Tom Clark to discuss the deal. All three men, along with their wives, met and had dinner at the Hotel Restaurant in my hometown of Ste. Genevieve, Missouri (currently called Hotel Audubon Grill and Bar). It was over dinner that the deal was discussed to include them as part of the Rokon team. As mentioned earlier, the 1973 Rokon team consisted of Jim Simmons, Stan Rubottom, Gary Snider, and Jim Fogle. Jim Fogle was no stranger to Jim and Stan. In fact, the two Jims had sort of a run-in the previous year.

Since there are a lot of Jims in this story, I will refer to them by their last names. In 1972, there was an enduro in Ohio called Little Burr. Simmons and Fogle were both riding in it. They had never met before this race. They were on a gravel road making up time, and Fogle overshot a turn. Simmons did, as well. As Fogle started to turn back, he did so right in front of Simmons, resulting in a crash. Fogle thought Simmons had broken his leg, but that wasn't the case. After the race, Simmons said Fogle came up to him to discuss the accident. The memorable, but less than ideal, introduction led to a lifelong friendship.

• • •

Here's some background on how Jim Fogle got into racing. Around 1965, Fogle bought a Honda 305 Scrambler. He could not remember if it was new or used or where or how he got it. He started riding with some friends, mostly on street bikes. Next thing they knew, he and his friends were riding along the railroad tracks and river bottoms. He then bought a Triumph T100, which was a 500cc bike in 1966, and started riding organized enduros. In 1969, Fogle bought a 360 Husqvarna and started racing both enduros and motocross. Fogle said there was a big difference in riding the Husqvarna versus the Triumph. There was a 300-pound difference but it was great training. Being from southern Ohio, the terrain was perfect for enduros. There would be 20–25 enduros a year right in Fogle's backyard.

At the time, Fogle, along with his late brother-in-law, started a motorcycle shop in Lithopolis, Ohio. Fogle worked on a guy's house in trade for a Hodaka and Maico dealership. Fogle also developed a friendship with John Penton through the enduro racing and eventually obtained a Penton and Husqvarna dealership from John. It was a great time to be in the enduro and motocross business, especially in Ohio.

Tom Clark, who only lived a few miles from Fogle in Ohio at the time, was working for Rokon in an effort to put an ISDT team together. Fogle and another Ohio native, Gary Snyder, got the call from Tom. That would have been in late 1972, so along with Jim Simmons and Stan Rubottom, team Rokon began. Fogle's Six Days history also included qualifying for the 1975 Isle of Man, where he earned bronze riding a Rokon and in 1977 Czechoslovakia he rode a KTM, but did not finish.

• • •

*T*he two-day qualifiers started out well for Jim and Stan in 1973. *The Daily Journal* headline was "Simmons And Clark Take Golds," and the article read:

> Local motorcycle riders scored well Saturday and Sunday in competition with national riders during the two-day endurance trials at Potosi, Missouri. There were 290 riders starting in the rain Saturday morning, with the field reduced to 109 Sunday morning, and only 92 riders finished. Bad weather took its toll of riders and motorcycles eliminated but is one of the purposes of the seven two-day events. Potosi was the second, of seven, qualifying endurance competitions which will determine who will represent the U.S. in the International Six-Days Trials this fall.
>
> Local riders Jim Simmons of Esther and Tom Clark of Potosi received gold medals at Potosi. Stan Rubottom of Esther, Jim Jones and Alan Rowe of Potosi, each received silver medals. Robert House of Bonne Terre and Gary Blair of Potosi received bronze medals.
>
> Malcolm Smith of California led the field of the top six overall riders followed by Tom Clark of Potosi in second place, Paul Berggren of Illinois third, Frank Piaseckis of Ohio fourth, Dick Mann of California fifth and Jack Penton of Ohio sixth.
>
> Motorcycle manufacturer's team competition for Penton in first place, Husqvarna second, Triumph third, Yankee (Ossa) fourth and Bultaco fifth.
>
> The Potosi Independent Riders finished in third position in the club team competition.
>
> Other notable Missouri riders who qualified for gold medals included Gary Surdyke of Festus, Ed Schmidt and Dave Mungenast from St. Louis.
>
> The next two-day qualifying trial event will be in Oregon in May.[12]

In all, the 1973 Rokon team fared well at the year's qualifying events. *The Daily Journal* reported:

> Motorcycle competition riders, Jim Simmons and Stan Rubottom of Esther, are among the first 88 riders who have qualified for positions on the United

(Previous) Jim Simmons 1973 at the Shamrock two-day qualifier. Photo by Jim Simmons
(Right) Jim Fogle racing his Rokon. Photo by Jim Fogle

(Left) Jim Simmons on his Rokon at a two-day qualifier. (Right) Jim Simmons preparing to start his Rokon at a two-day qualifier. Photos by Jim Simmons

States teams for the ISDT. The international competition is being held in the United States for the first time and will occur late this fall.

Tom Clark, American Motorcyclist Association District Representative at Potosi and Ed Schmidt of St. Louis had already been qualified by past performances but have also compiled impressive point standings during the four qualifying events already held this year. Other area riders now qualified include Dave Mungenast of St. Louis and Gary Surdyke of Festus.

Selection points earned by individual riders in a series of six two-day trials are being used to gauge performance and establish team placements. To date, after the first four qualifying events, a hypothetically perfect rider who won every event and was consistently highest in the special tests would have 900 selection points.

Of the trophy and Vase A team members, Ed Schmidt has 969.5 points and Tom Clark has 992.4 points. Jim Simmons is close behind the leaders with just 1012.2 points, while Rubottom is further down the listing, but ahead of Mungenast.

Leading U.S. riders is performance points are Jack Penton with 918.5 and Malcolm Smith with 918.6 points. Malcolm Smith was the star of the motion picture *On Any Sunday*, but is primarily a strong competitor and motorcycle rider.

The U.S. Teams are to be selected from the 235 riders who have set out to enter the six qualifying competitions, one of which was held at Potosi this spring.[13]

(Right) Jim Simmons on his Rokon at a two-day qualifier. Photo by Jim Simmons

Around the time that article came out, bad luck would put Stan out of ISDT contention. While competing at the Bad Rock qualifier in Weston, Oregon, Stan broke his collarbone. To this day, the Rokon motorcycle haunts him. He never really cared for the bike. The qualifier before Bad Rock was at Trask Mountain in McMinnville, Oregon. It was at this qualifier Stan and Fogle both experienced carburetor issues at high altitudes, and both lost a lot of time diagnosing the problem. Motorcycle issues during a qualifier can be most frustrating when you are as competitive as these guys are. Equipment failures kept a lot of good riders from achieving their goals. Jim Simmons, Jim Fogle, and Gary Snider would go on to represent the USA and Rokon at the 1973 ISDT in Dalton, Massachusetts. All three would medal, along with individual rider Ron LaMastus. Rokon ended up winning a special Engineering Achievement Award, as well.

An interesting story about the two Jims during the Six Days in 1973: According to Simmons, during the race, on the fifth day, Fogle's frame cracked between the steering neck and the down tube. Fogle noticed his wheelbase getting longer. They saw the crack at a gas stop. According to Simmons, he rarely ever carried money with him during a race, but that day he had $20 in his pocket. Simmons rode ahead to look for help, which he found at a farmhouse just off the route. The owners were sitting outside watching the race, and they had the door to their workshop open. Simmons pulled in and asked if they had a welder handy. They pointed to the workshop. As Fogle approached the farmhouse, Simmons flagged him in and proceeded to weld up Fogle's frame. Simmons slipped the farmer the $20 and away they went. Both riders finished out the sixth day and medaled. Simmons says that Fogle still owes him the $20 from that day.

The next year, 1974, would bring on more challenges for the pair. Stan received a call from Rokon to see if he'd like to be back on the team. Bad memories were still fresh in Stan's mind, so he passed. After a few days of kicking it around, he called Rokon back, having a change of heart. But, by then, Rokon already had a full team. The 1974 Rokon team consisted of Jim Simmons, Jim Fogle, Jim Hollander, Gary Snider, and Dave Mungenast. This would be the year they coined the phrase "The Three Jims." Not to be discouraged by his decision, Stan reached out to his friends at St. Louis Honda and picked up a Husqvarna to compete on during the 1974 season. Although both Jim and Stan gave it their all during the qualifying rounds in 1974, they both missed the cut to represent the USA at the ISDT in Camerino, Italy.

Another story that Fogle remembered was the two-day qualifiers at Potosi in 1974. Fogle had gotten hurt and couldn't go on, while Simmons' bike broke and could not be fixed. They both were racing their Rokons. They ended up swapping number plates out on the trail, and Simmons finished on Fogle's bike. No one found out and Simmons took a silver at the event.

In 1974, on another trip down to Picayune, Mississippi for a two-day qualifier, Jim and his friends showed up early. They pulled into a restaurant for breakfast before the big race. It was closed, and there was no other place around to eat. Luckily, a local drunk stumbled out of a car parked in the same lot and told them to go inside and make themselves at home. They found an unlocked door at the back of the building and proceeded to go in. The wives cooked breakfast for the group. As they were finishing up, the owner arrived. Apparently, the night

On September 17, 1973, the Rokon factory team started a six day journey carrying them 1000 miles through the toughest terrain possible, the 48th International Six Days Trial, better known as the Olympics of Motorcycling

On September 22, this same team crossed the finish line, tired but successful. Jim Simmons had earned a bronze medal, Gary Snider a silver medal and Jim Fogle a bronze medal. In addition, the team brought home a special award — the Engineering Achievement Award, a 1st in 48 years of I.S.D.T. competition.

— Engineered and Manufactured —
ROKON, INC • 160 Emera d Street • Keene, New Hampshire 03431 • (603) 352-7341

Team Rokon at the start of the 1973 ISDT. Photo by Rokon International, Inc

before, the owner's wife had given birth to twins, so he couldn't open the restaurant as early as usual. The group thought they would get the cops called on them, but the owner was fine with it. They paid for their meals and went on to the race.

The only member of the Rokon team to qualify for the USA in 1974 was Jim Hollander. Due to a bad accident at the Shamrock qualifier, Dave Mungenast missed making it on the USA team, but was able to catch a ride on the Canadian team with his Rokon. Not to be discouraged, Jim and Stan's competitive nature brought them back the following year, hungrier than ever.

In 1975, Jim and Stan set out to go all the way, but things didn't start out so smoothly. With Jim still riding for the Rokon team and Stan still riding his Husqvarna, they headed to the first qualifier in Forked River, New Jersey. With fifty miles to go, Jim had an accident and broke his

SILVER AND GOLD MEDAL WINNERS Stan Rubottom (L) and Jim Simmons (R) of Esther who finished the two-day motorcycle trials at Potosi among the national leaders. Carpet installation experts by trade, the two are hopeful of winning berths on the ROKON factory team for the ISDT in September. They finished well at Ft. Hood and Potosi with the next trials to be held in Oregon in May.

(Previous) Rokon riders Gary Snider, Jim Fogle, Jim Simmons, Mike DiPrete, and Ron LaMastus 1973 ISDT. Photo by Jim Simmons (Above) Jim and Stan Daily Journal photo from 1974. Photo by The Daily Journal

leg. He managed to finish the qualifier and stay on a gold medal pace. Stan said afterward, even wearing a cast, Jim was doing things he shouldn't have been doing, but he managed to heal up enough to still qualify for the USA team by winning gold at four other qualifiers. Their local newspaper, *The Daily Journal*, gave the two riders some well-deserved recognition:

Jim Simmons and Stan Rubottom are quite proficient in their sport. They are motorcycle racers. And, if things go right, they could be representing the United States in the ISDT on the Isle of Man, Great Britain, this October.

Simmons and Rubottom, both of Esther, each won gold medals at the Ozark two-day trial, held at Potosi on May 31-June 1. For Jim, it was his fifth gold medal in six trials. Stan won his fourth gold out of six trial runs.

"They (AMA) take your best four events of the seven qualifying runs," Rubottom said of the standards to qualify for the United States team. "That means our best four runs are gold medals."

Rubottom and Simmons have been attempting to qualify for the trials for the past 5 years. In 1973, Simmons made the six-day trials, riding for a Rokon manufacturer's team. He finished 18th overall in his engine classification. Simmons rides a 340-cubic inch Rokon.

"I ride a 250-cc Husqvarna," Rubottom said. "The bike fits my size. Jim is bigger than I am, so he rides a bigger bike."

"We really got into motorcycles just for pleasure," Simmons said, explaining how the pair began their competitive efforts. "We each bought a bike to ride on camping trips. We bought small bikes and ran them down at Mine LaMotte lake one day. After that, we traded them off for bigger bikes."

Both Simmons and Rubottom have entered competitive riding relatively late. But they have done extremely well in a demanding sport.

"Our work helps us stay in shape," Simmons said of the training the two do. They are employed by the Brown Carpet Co., Esther, as carpet layers. "We both were in sports in high school and in college, and we lift some weights to keep in shape. But riding keeps you in shape also."

Dangerous Sport: "This really is a dangerous sport," Simmons said. "A lot of kids riding bikes don't realize that."

To clarify, he told of the injuries he and Rubottom had sustained during trail competitions. Simmons has suffered a broken leg and Rubottom a foot injury and a shoulder injury.

"You really have to concentrate all the time," Rubottom said. "You're riding a bike sometimes in narrow paths, just wide enough for your handlebars to clear, and you really have to think ahead of yourself."

"I've thought a lot about the time I broke my leg," Simmons said. He suffered the injury in the year's first qualifying trials in New Jersey. "I can't remember what I hit, but I know that I wasn't concentrating on what I was doing. It gets hard to concentrate when you ride for 10 hours by yourself."

Fortunately for Simmons, he had almost two months to recover from the injury. But it did not keep him from finishing the trials.

"I was about fifty miles from the finish," he said. "So, I got up and finished the race. I won a gold medal."

Gold medals are awarded to riders who finish within 15 percent of the fastest rider's time on the course and in other special trials.

"They have acceleration and other tests," Rubottom said. "Each has a certain amount of points for the performance. Those tests are tabulated with the run speed for a final score. At the end of the race, also, the headlight and taillight on the bike must work."

Simmons, riding on the Rokon factory team, usually only gets to see his bike in time to test it on Fridays before the race. He may not even get the chance to do so then, because he might arrive after the bikes are impounded before the race.

"I've been fortunate to have Jim here," Rubottom said. "Otherwise, it really would be expensive."

Also, Wayne Gibson of Bonne Terre and Jim's brother, Gene, have gone to some of the trials with the two. They split the driving time usually non-stop to the event, which could be halfway across the continent or help by hauling gasoline for the bikes to the refueling areas.

The trials are difficult cross-country racing events, with the special tests added to further determine the quality of the machine.

The ISDT were held in Great Britain as a test of motorcycles. The event was dominated for a while by the Britons. The teams of Czechoslovakia now have been leaders in the six-day competitions. United States participation has become serious only recently.

Eight two-day trials are held in the United States to qualify riders for the American team. The Potosi event is one of those.

"I think that the Ft. Hood (Texas) trial was the toughest we have been on this year," Simmons said. "It was run on the Army base there, and it was covered with tank trails and some pretty rough country. You do get to see some beautiful country, though," he said. "We've been from coast to coast, north to south. The trials are held on some places that you would never see from a car."

Both men agree that the trials are an equal test of machine and man. Riders from other types of motorcycling have tried to master trials riding, but it is different from either enduro or flat track racing.

Riders are allowed to take certain mechanical equipment along with them on the race to make repairs on bikes. Other parts of the machines are marked to prevent repairs.

"You can replace a broken handlebar, or repair a flat tire, but some of the major stuff cannot be replaced," Rubottom said. "The riders don't get a lot of time either. Repairs must be completed during the race."

Races are usually run at a pace speed of 24 miles per hour. That figure may be changed depending on weather and course conditions before the first rider of the day leaves the line.

"There is no substitute for experience in this type of racing," Simmons said. "You have to know your machine and what it's capable of doing. You can take a good machine and an inexperienced rider and he can't do it."

Rubottom does his own bike work, since he is an independent rider. Simmons, as a member of the Rokon team, has his bike worked on by the factory personnel. Both agree that it is important to know what the machine is like before running it.

There is one more qualifying trial for the six-day team, but neither Simmons or Rubottom plan to go to the event, at Hannibal, N.Y., this weekend.

"I'm not going to New York," Rubottom said, "because there isn't anything, I can do to improve my position. They take your best four events, and I've got four gold medals."

The team will be composed of 30 riders, and Stan and Jim estimate that only 15 men have four gold medals so far in the qualifying runs.

Jim Simmons racing the Fort Hood two-day qualifier in 1975. Photo by Coy Hopson

Team USA at the opening ceremony of the 1976 ISDT. Photo by Wayne Gibson

Both Simmons and Rubottom feel that they have a spot on the team. But neither are counting on a trip to the Isle of Man yet.

When the October trials come up, however, Stan Rubottom and Jim Simmons plan to be wearing the United States' Team colors.[14]

Shortly after that article was published, both Jim and Stan learned that they made the USA ISDT team to compete at the Isle of Man. The Rokon ISDT team for 1975 included Jim Hollander, Jim Simmons, Ron Bishop, and alternates were Jim Fogle and Dave Mungenast. A local benefit poker run was held to help fund Stan's cost for travel. Stan was selected as a member of the South Penn Enduro Riders club, along with Ken Maahs and Chris Carter. Making it to compete to the ISDT is one thing, but completing the race is another, and 1975 wasn't a good year for Jim or Stan.

While competing in the Isle of Man ISDT, Jim and Stan had a round of bad luck. For Stan, after competing for three days, he twisted his knee and pulled some ligaments, which kept him from finishing the last three days. Jim made it to day four, holding a gold medal pace, but then damaged the magnesium front rim on his Rokon. The officials would not allow him to continue due to safety concerns. Jim said there was about a six-inch chunk of magnesium missing from his front rim, and you could see the red inner tube, which didn't help hide the damage.

Jim was knocked on the head pretty hard during the accident as well, leaving him dizzy and not all there. He was coming into a right-hand turn when his bike hit the berm on his left side. It pitched him about twenty feet. As he slowly got up, he noticed a few spectators run over and pick up the bike. Jim mounted his Rokon and followed the next rider to the finish line.

Jim Simmons tried desperately to fix a front wheel, but the officials declared it unsafe and refused to let him go on.

Dirt Rider *magazine photo of Jim after his accident at the 1975 ISDT. Caption says it all. Photo from Hi-Torque Publications, Inc.*

Refusing to be discouraged by the outcome of the 1975 ISDT, Jim and Stan set out to qualify again in 1976. Both riders took four gold medals. *The Daily Journal* had this to say:

For the second consecutive year, Jim Simmons and Stan Rubottom will be representing the United States in the ISDT. This year's event will be held Sept. 20–26 in Zeltweg, Austria.

"We are getting everything together," Simmons said. "We are enthused about going." Simmons is the veteran of the pair of riders from Esther. Both men work together at Brown Carpet Co.

Simmons has made two previous trips but will be riding a different bike on his third trip. In the past, Rokon has supplied the machine, but this year Husqvarna will be furnishing the motorcycle from its factory.

On Simmons' two previous trips, he cracked a rim after four days in the 1975 Trials on the Isle of Man, Great Britain. In 1973, he won a bronze medal in the six-day Trials held in Massachusetts.

"That was the only time the trials have been held in the United States," Simmons said. Simmons qualified with four gold medals in his four qualifying runs. He won gold medals in American trials in California, Alabama, Texas and New Jersey.

"A lot can happen in six days," Simmons said. "It takes a lot of preparation and a lot of luck. Hopefully, we should do well."

As for Rubottom, one thinks he would hope for better luck than he endured in the 1975 Trials. He rode three days before injuring a leg and missed the final three days.

"I'm looking forward to going," Rubottom said. "It will be a lot tougher this year. Last year, it rained. Also, the competition gets stiffer each year."

Rubottom has also switched cycles from last year and has changed to riding a Yamaha. He rode a Husqvarna last year. This year's Yamaha will be one of four such bikes that is being prepared for the trials.

Rubottom qualified with gold medals in Alabama, Texas, Michigan and New Jersey.

"We will be pretty close to the site of the Winter Olympics (Innsbruck)," Rubottom said. "It will be mountainous terrain and it will be a well-organized run."

It takes concentration, skill and determination to do well in the sport of motorcycling, especially at the level of competition that this pair will be competing against.[15]

As mentioned earlier, Jim raced the qualifiers on a Rokon but switched to Husqvarna before the ISDT due to Rokon cutting all support. Going into Austria, Jim's bike still needed fine-tuning. It was fitted with a Mikuni carburetor, just like the Husqvarnas of Dick Burleson and Malcolm Smith were running that year, but it still needed to be jetted correctly. Time did not allow for this. Jim said he lost out on winning a gold medal the first day of the 1976 ISDT when his Husqvarna seized. Going into the first day, he wasn't feeling very confident of the jetting of his Mikuni carburetor and, sure enough, his feelings proved correct. Once his

(Previous left) Stan Rubottom #339 at the 1976 ISDT. (Previous right) Jim Simmons #319 at the 1976 ISDT. (Above) Jim Simmons #319 at the 1976 ISDT. (Below) Lars Larsson #185 at the 1976 ISDT. Photos by Wayne Gibson

bike seized, he had to stop and allow the engine to cool down to break it free. Once he got the motor running again, he spent the next five days taking it easy and babying the bike, as to not destroy the motor. Jim's friend, Tony Budde, said, "You knew it was Jim's bike coming before you could see him. The top end of his bike was making a horrible sound."

A *Cycle News* article read: "Simmons' bike seized on the first day on the road, then it stuck twice more on the third day. Jim raised the needle a notch, found a way to catch up with the course, and was able to salvage a silver medal."[16]

Jim said that fellow rider Dick Mann was attending the ISDT as a support person and was stationed along the route in a basement garage of a house. Word was that Dick was swapping out pistons for people if they needed one. The only problem with this was you had to cut the tamper proof inspection seal that was between the head and the cylinder to swap out a piston. Doing this would cost you points—or even the race—and would have knocked Jim out of medal contention. Jim decided against swapping out his piston and to baby his bike along. His efforts proved good enough for a silver medal. Just think, if Jim's bike were jetted properly, he would have won a gold with no problem. Stan just missed out on a gold medal, as well, in Austria when he was racing his Yamaha IT400 support bike. As he was finishing up his run, he tangled with fellow Yamaha rider John Fero. The time lost trying to untangle the bikes cost Stan a gold medal.

Cycle News reported on Stan's accident: "I've been riding just barely on Gold," Stan said when we talked on the morning of the fourth day, "but I wish I could build up a cushion." Stan, riding a prototype of the 1977 Yamaha IT400, tangled with fellow Yamaha rider John Fero during the sixth day MX special test. The two bikes locked together, taking several minutes to pull them apart, and the time lost' cost Stan his Gold.[17]

I could not find much information on Jim and Stan's ISDT racing efforts in 1977, but what I did stumble across were answers to questions that arose during the preservation. The multiple-colored inspection paint marks, newer dated rear Sun rim, box of spare parts, and the extra exhaust that came with Jim's bike, all were figured out. In my mind, the preservation wasn't finished until all questions were answered. Thanks to the online archives of *Cycle News*, I was able to find my answers.

I focused my *Cycle News* research after the 1976 ISDT and found that, in 1977, Jim raced the Husqvarna while being sponsored by Cycle East during the ISDT qualifying rounds in the United States. Rich Burleson was also part of this team. Cycle East was discussed earlier and was the name on one of the jerseys Jim gave me. Jim used the Husqvarna to race qualifiers and a few national enduros in 1977, which explains the multiple inspection marks found on his bike.

At the Maplesville, Alabama two-day qualifier in 1977, the Cycle East team of Burleson—Bob Popiel and Jim Simmons—were the club team winners. Unfortunately, Jim did not qualify for the ISDT in 1977. It had come down to one of the last qualifiers in Oregon, Trask Mountain. Jim had to place high in this race to qualify but, during the race, his rear wheel was pierced by a railroad spike. Unable to continue, Jim's hopes for the 1977 ISDT were over. After the Trask Mountain qualifier, he had Donelson motorcycle dealership in Park Hills fit a

Stan Rubottom and John Fero's incident. Photo by Wayne Gibson

new rear Sun rim, hence the 1977 date on the Sun rim on Jim's bike. The extra exhaust pipe I had was a Husqvarna CR model pipe that he used in 1977. This would be the last season Jim would race the Husqvarna.

The 1978 season would be Jim and Stan's last year of competitive racing. It started out with them getting support from Yamaha. An article in *Cycle News* read:

> Carl Cranke, Chris Carter, Jeff Hammond, Stan Rubottom, Jim Simmons and Dennis Reese have been chosen to ride 400cc Yamahas in the ISDT Qualifiers. Mike Deyo, Mark Deyo, David Ashley, and Ken Maahs will be mounted on 250cc machines. Dwight Rudder and Ken Harvey have agreed to pilot the 175cc models. The Yamaha ISDT deal includes bikes, some spare parts and for those who qualify for the '78 ISDT, a ticket to Sweden. No support crew has been organized. It's a rider assistance program similar to Yamaha's MX Support

(Previous left top) Billy Uhl at the 1976 ISDT. (Previous left bottom) Carl Cranke #305 at the 1976 ISDT. (Previous right top) Al Eames with Jim Simmons in the background wearing his Mungenast Dirt Bike Headquarters jacket 1976 ISDT. (Previous right bottom) Bike impound at the 1976 ISDT. Photos by Wayne Gibson

Coordinator, who's putting it all together. By the way, don't bother sending in resumes if you think you may belong on Ruben Portillo's team. He's already chosen his men and is just waiting on their confirmation before releasing more names.[18]

Jim and Stan, although they put in a solid effort, didn't qualify for the 1978 USA ISDT team. Jim, thanks to Lars Larsson, was able to go as a Mexico team member. Because of the switch, Jim could not use his Yamaha IT support bike that he was racing on all of 1978. He found himself again without a bike to compete on for the ISDT. He turned to his friend Carl Donelson of Donelson Cycles, for help. Jim said Carl told him he could get him a bike, but he'd have to drive up to a Yamaha warehouse in Chicago to pick it up. Unlike his experience with his Husqvarna, when Jim arrived to pick up his ISDT bike, a fully assembled leftover 1977 Yamaha YZ400 was there waiting for him. The only thing Jim added to the bike was a bigger IT model gas tank. He couldn't thank Carl enough.

Jim in Sweden 1978 racing for Mexico on his Donelson supplied 1977 Yamaha YZ400. Photo by Fred Cameron

(Above) 1978 Sweden ISDT sign. (Below) Jim Simmons up close. Team Mexico. Photos by Fred Cameron

The Donelson Influence

I had the honor to sit down with Carl Donelson to discuss his history and influence on the local riding scene. Carl was a rider and business owner. Sometimes it's hard to do both, especially when you have three dealerships and catalog sales to manage. Carl did have a few racing stories to share that related to my ISDT research. He rode in the Potosi, Missouri two-day qualifier. He was on a team with Robert Civy and Rob Harris. He rode a 1966 BSA 441, while the two Robs rode Yamahas. It was a rough event and, after the first day, Carl told Robert and Rob that he was going to go home. They said, "Oh no, you'll ruin the team. You'll need to come and finish the race tomorrow." So, Carl drove over to stay at Gale and Ann Halbrook's house (they ran the Donelson Dealership in Flat River, Missouri). Carl stayed the night, got up in the morning, went back to the race, and rode the whole event. When he finished, he found his teammates all dressed in street clothes. Carl asked the guys what had happened, and they said, "Oh, well, we were too beat up, so we didn't ride." Obviously, the team didn't do well.

Carl raced everything from enduros to flat track. He wanted to flat track race more than anything, but when he found it was going to be difficult to succeed at it, he decided to stick with his business and his family. He made the right decision. Dick Mann was a good friend of Carl's, and he told Carl it took him seven years to learn how to race. Dick, in Carl's opinion, is the best motorcycle rider in the world, so for a man like that to tell him it took several years.... He's glad he didn't do it.

There would never have been a Flat River Grand Prix if it wasn't for Gale Halbrook and Carl. It was Gale's idea and Carl helped put it in motion. The 100-mile race was pitched to the Flat River Chamber of Commerce as a fund raiser for the city. The event started in 1982 and ran through 1998. In its day, it was the largest off-road motorcycle race east of the Rocky Mountains, drawing over 750 entries. It was held at St. Joe State Park.

Carl and Dave Mungenast were friends way before they were in business. Carl started his business in 1962, and Dave started his in 1965. Dave started at Bob Shultz on Locust Street, where Carl frequented. They've been friends since 1958. Carl would rent Dave's Doe Run Cycle Park for an employee and customer appreciation day. He said over 2,500 people attended.

Carl said Tom Clark was the original showoff, but he could back it up. He was very good on a motorcycle. When Carl became a Yamaha dealership, Tom Clark was the East Coast sales manager who ran the Cherry Hill, New Jersey, operation from 1962–1963. He flat tracked for a while and was a BSA roadman, but he was fired because he would only visit the dealers that

Poster of the 1988 Flat River Grand Prix. Photo by Carl Donelson

were on the way to the racetracks. Carl said Tom could ride a trials bike better than anyone he had ever seen.

Carl first met Jim and Stan back in the 1960s. Carl's best memory of Jim was when he was on his Rokon. "Jim would start that bike like he was starting a weed eater." Carl remembers seeing Jim motocross that Rokon at the Cedar Falls MX track. "It was amazing how fast he could ride that motorcycle with no gear box—it was an automatic. Stan was a little more reserved. Not as flamboyant as Jim, but a good rider, though," Carl said. It was at one of Carl's yearly racer parties in 2019 when I first got to meet ISDT medalist Chris Carter.

The Carter Connection

Chris Carter's name came up a several times during my conversations with Jim and Stan. He was in a lot of Stan's off-road motorcycle magazines advertising his company, Motion Pro. Carter's name also came up when talking with Kevin Hagerty that dealt with Chris test riding here in Missouri and his ISDT history with Yamaha. So, it's funny how I ran into him while attending Carl Donelson's annual racer party in 2019. I introduced myself and quickly tied in my relationship with Jim and Stan. I was very familiar with the products Chris' company sold, but I didn't know the story behind Chris' history in off-road racing. I took it upon myself to find out.

Chris Carter's involvement with Yamaha and off-road racing stems back to 1970 when he was working at Ray Abram's motorcycle shop called A&A Motors in Redwood City, California. At that time, Chris was motocross racing Maicos. Ray was good friends with the new race director of Yamaha, Pete Schick. In 1972, when Yamaha came out with a small run of DT2MX prototypes, Chris was selected to race one. Throughout 1972, Chris traveled and raced with the likes of Gary and Don Jones, but soon he realized motocross racing wasn't his strong suit. Off-road racing was more his style. That's when Bill Stewart came into the picture.

According to an article in *Cycle Magazine*, Stewart was a self-taught motorcycle technician:

> After leaving his home in Indiana at the age of 17, Bill enrolled in the University of Nevada and finished his education at the University of Oregon as a graduate in forestry. After three years with the U.S. Department of Forestry he bought a motorcycle shop in Redwood City, California. From 1960 to 1966 Bill sold and serviced BSA, Greeves, Suzuki, Jawa/CZ and whatever else moved on two wheels. Bill started riding in enduros around Redwood City and was 25 when he rode his first competition event. In 1964, Bill acquired his FIM license through some underground sources and competed in the East German hosted ISDT for factory Jawa as the B-Vase team. Bill would finish with a silver medal.
>
> Bill closed his business and moved to Reno for a job with Yamaha in the late 1960's to work on the development of the Yamaha DT1 project. His previous racing experience made him a perfect fit for the job. Fast forward to 1973 and Bill was now in charge of the Yamaha IT development group. In mid-1973 Bill reached out to Chris to see if he'd be interested in helping with the IT development group. Chris was a rider for hire.[19]

The early IT bikes used the dual shock YZ360 as a test bed for development. All development work was done in-house. Mark Porter, Bill Stewart, John Volkman, and Kevin Hagerty were all members of the development team. From 1973–1974, Chris raced a modified Yamaha MX360 with Maico forks and did a lot of testing in the Mojave Desert. Then, in 1975, Yamaha entered Chris into the California City ISDT qualifier—also known as the "Shamrock"—on a modified MX400 Monoshock bike. This would be the first public display of the IT prototype.

After the first race, Chris didn't know what was to happen next with Yamaha, until one day he received a call telling him to race a qualifier down at Fort Hood, Texas. At Fort Hood, they modified the tank on Chris' bike. They took two MX/YZ aluminum tanks, cut and stacked them to make a larger capacity tank. They welded them together, but they also sealed the tank to prevent any leaks. This all worked fine for preventing leaks, but it gave Chris problems. On day one, the sealer started coming loose and it clogged the petcock. Luckily, Chris identified the problem quickly and finished the two-day.

Chris raced that bike at all the two-day qualifiers in 1975, reporting back to Yamaha after each one with things that worked and things that didn't work. At the qualifier in Potosi, Missouri, the rear sub frame broke. They had to cut the sub frame off with a hacksaw. Everything behind his seat was missing. This happened on the last day, and there was a motocross test coming up. Luckily, with Chris' motocross background, this test was his favorite. It also helped that the Yamahas would start in gear, so Chris would always get the hole shot during dead engine starts. He won the MX test and was ready for the ISDT.

A new bike was built for Chris for the 1975 Isle of Man ISDT. It used an oversized plastic gas tank. He experienced some ignition problems throughout the race. He also had to push start the bike for the last road race special test, but he finished the six days and became the only Japanese bike to finish at the Isle of Man that year. He received a bronze medal in 1975. That bike then got shipped back to Japan.

In 1976, Yamaha released the IT models with plastic tanks. A three-rider team was assembled for the 1976 Austria ISDT consisting of Chris Carter, John Fero, and Dave Ashley. These riders were furnished with a Bill-Stewart-modified-production Yamaha ITs. According to an article in *Cycle Magazine*, the following modifications were performed just six weeks before the ISDT in Austria:

- The spark arrestor was replaced with a YZ silencer.
- The carburetor received the YZ jetting.
- Preston Petty headlight number plate and fender with taillight were added.
- Stock wiring rerouted to prevent pinching or crimping.
- Seat shortened 3 inches to make room for tool pouch.
- Counter shaft sprocket cover trimmed down for mud clearance.
- Foot pegs drilled out to prevent mud caking.
- Leather tool pouch installed behind seat.
- Fork dampening modified and accumulators added.
- Speedo drive was removed.

Chris Carter at the Fort Hood two-day qualifier. Note his newly fabricated oversized aluminum gas tank. Photo by Coy Hopson

- O-ring chain added.
- Front brake cable safety wired to brake plate.
- Foot brake adjuster modified.
- Webco choke knob added to carburetor.
- New chain adjuster wear block added.
- Center stands fitted to bikes.
- Rear brake adjuster modified for quick removal.
- Chain adjusters modified for quicker chain adjustments.
- Both rims turned down on one side to speed tire changes.
- Rear brake plate swapped for aluminum with welded on spacer.
- Head pipe tension springs modified for clearance.
- Magura levers and aluminum handlebars added.
- Air box mods to improve filter positioning.[20]

During the course of the Austria ISDT, Chris would have his throttle stick while riding through the infield grass track. This caused him to hit a spectator. It was Rod Bush's mother, and the collision broke her hip. Up until Rod passed away, he would always introduce Chris as the guy who put his mother in the hospital. The team of three Yamaha ISDT riders all won gold medals. Chris secured his gold by winning the last motocross special test of the race.

In 1977, Chris would qualify for the ISDT in Czechoslovakia. It was known as one of the toughest ISDTs ever. Rainstorms caused Chris to hour out by one minute at the last checkpoint on the fifth day of the ISDT. The following year, his two-day qualifier participation would be limited by injury.

Chris' association with Yamaha made it easier to attend qualifiers. He was flown to all the races. He also got his bikes and parts for free and received paid time away from work and mileage. After 1978, Chris retired from ISDT competition. He left Rocky Cycles in 1984 to start his company, Motion Pro. I would learn shortly after meeting Chris that we had a mutual friend in common, Rex Marsee, an engineer on the Harley-Davidson MX development team who I would become friends with while researching and preserving the #49 Harley-Davidson team bike.

Chris Carter, Bill Stewart, and Mark Porter after the 1975 Potosi two-day qualifier. Notice the missing rear subframe and spliced gas tank. This would be the last time Chris raced the bike. Photo by Chris Carter

Finishing Touches

*T*he time had come when the Jim Simmons' bike was finally finished. I tried fitting the speedo that I received from Stan, but it just didn't seem right. I had more photos of the bike without the speedo, so I decided to leave it off. I took some clear lacquer paint and placed a couple coats on all the inspection marks to help them hang on for future generations to see. I got this tip from Jeff Debell. To highlight the event, I parked the bike and surrounded it with all of Jim's items he entrusted to me. I hung his jerseys in the background and placed his trophies, toolbox, and gear around the bike. This made for an excellent photo that told the story of Jim's riding career. There was the Jack Pine trophy Jim won to become an A-Class rider, his USA helmet that he wore during his first ISDT in 1973, and his Mexico ISDT helmet that he wore when he ended his ISDT career in 1978. For these items to come together after forty years and to be in the shape they are in is a miracle.

Now that Jim's bike was complete, my goal was to get some pictures of him with the bike. What better way to do it than to have his riding buddies present. I reached out to Ray Mungenast and mentioned how I would love to get a photo of Ed Schmidt and Jim with the bike they put together forty-two years earlier. Without hesitation, Ray said, "Why don't you plan that meeting at the museum?" Ray's family museum is one of the best motorcycle museums to visit in St. Louis. Not only did Ray allow me to display my Harley-Davidson MX team bike at the museum for their 2018 Supercross party, but now he's allowing me to celebrate the completion of Jim Simmons' ISDT Husqvarna there. This is an invitation you do not refuse.

Around this time, I was finishing up the Malcolm Smith book that Jim gave me and also reviewing the photos that I received from Tony Budde and Wayne Gibson. There was one photo from the Austria ISDT that had Jim, Malcolm, and a woman they called "Honda Mary" in it. She would later become Malcolm's wife. Feeling really into Malcolm's book and knowing I had some photos he'd never seen before, I took it upon myself to email his dealership to see if they would share the photos with him and tell him my story of Jim's bike. To my surprise, Malcolm emailed me back. Talk about being on cloud nine.

His email read:

Keith, thanks for the pictures you sent me. The Husqvarna you restored looks good. We have a museum of old bikes at our store. People come to the store and say they know I like old Husqvarnas and just give them to me. Most of them are very rough and not running. We have maybe twenty-three or so. I need to find parts to restore them. Honda Mary came to California and we lived together for two years then got married for three or so years before separating. Happily married now for 36 years with current wife. Malcolm Smith – still riding for fun!

(Above) Left hand view of Jim Simmons' 1976 ISDT Husqvarna preserved for all to see.
(Below) Right hand view of Jim Simmons' 1976 ISDT Husqvarna preserved for all to see. Photos by Keith Geisner

With the 2018 Christmas season just around the corner, I decided to plan the event at the museum in early 2019. At the time, the date worked for Jim, the museum, and Ed Schmidt, but as the date quickly approached, Ed had to cancel due to other arrangements. In his place, his sons, Ed Jr. and Pat, attended the event. Also, Stan Rubottom did not know if he was going to be able to make it. This would not be a celebration if the two friends could not be together, I thought.

The gathering went well, even though the weather did not cooperate. Jim showed up early with friends Tony Budde and Wayne Gibson. I was joined by my father, wife, and father-in-law. Soon enough, my uncle's childhood riding buddy, Wayne Kertz, showed up, and then Tim Hamilton. Before long, we had a room full of people telling stories and reminiscing about the past. A little later, Stan Rubottom came walking in and surprised us all. Seeing Stan made my day.

The bike was under heavy inspection by everyone. To say I was a little nervous was an understatement. The Schmidt brothers gave it a thumbs-up and confirmed the brake light switch that was noted in the photos. At this point, I explained what I uncovered about the multiple-colored inspection marks from the 1977 qualifiers, so this confirmed Ray's initial observation that the bike was raced more than the Six Days event in Austria. All in all, the museum event was a success.

Jim Simmons, Malcolm Smith, and Honda Mary in Austria 1976. Photo by Tony Budde

• • •

A few months later, in April 2019, we flew out to California to attend the Trailblazers Motorcycle Club banquet. The Trailblazers

Jim Simmons, Malcolm Smith, and Honda Mary in Austria 1976. Photo by Wayne Gibson

hold this annual banquet to induct riders into their Hall of Fame. This was their seventy-fifth anniversary hosting the event. Not only was Rex Staten of the Harley-Davidson MX team getting inducted, but so was John Penton. Was there a chance I could meet John Penton in person? I was hoping so! Also, there was a good chance Malcolm Smith would be there, since he was already a member of the Trailblazers Hall of Fame.

(Left top) Left to right: Dave Mungenast Jr., Stan Rubottom, Ray Mungenast, and Jim Simmons.
(Left bottom) Left to right: Stan Rubottom, Jim Simmons, Dave Larsen, Wayne Gibson, and Tony Budde.
(Above) Left to right: Pat Schmidt, Jim Simmons, Ed. Schmidt Jr., and Stan Rubottom. Photos by Keith Geisner

I brought extra number plates and permanent markers just in case I would have a chance at any autographs. As soon as we entered the front doors to the hotel, I noticed John Penton and his family seated in the lobby. My heart skipped a beat. I quickly checked in and then ran out to the car to tell my wife, Sara, the news. She didn't get my excitement, but she played along as I approached the Pentons for autographs. Jeff, Tom, Jack, and John all signed my number plate and posed for pictures with me. Carl Cranke, Lars Larsson, Chris Carter, and Eric Jenson were also in the lobby, and they autographed my number plate, as well. Of course, I brought photos of Jim and Stan along to break the ice. It was awesome to meet the founding member of the 1978 Mexico team, Lars Larsson. Lars looked at Jim's photo and said, "There's Mexican Jim!" Everyone was so nice and treated me like one of their peers. Little did they know, I was in heaven. I also ran into Paul Stannard, of Preston Petty Products, on the elevator. He saw my handful of number plates and asked if those were Preston Petty number plates. I was like a deer in the headlights because the plates I had were old school, K&N brand. I apologized and made a mental note to never make that mistake again.

The next day after the bike show, Sara and I sat and spoke with Carl Crank briefly. I discussed my ties with Jim, Stan and Ray. Carl spoke highly of Ray's dad, Dave Sr., and told us about his life and family achievements after racing. That night at the Trailblazers' banquet dinner, I was able to introduce myself to Malcolm Smith and get his signature on the same number plate as the rest of the ISDT members. To be among that group of riders after researching and reading about them over the last year meant so much. I'm very thankful I had the opportunity to meet them all in person.

A number plate full of gold medal signatures to remind me of this special trip. Photo by Keith Geisner

I was blessed to get a photo with the Penton family at the 2019 Trailblazer banquet. Photo by Keith Geisner

ISDT legends Lars Larsson, Jeff Penton, and Tom Penton. Photo by Keith Geisner

I had the honor of meeting Chris Carter for a second time at the 2019 Trailblazer banquet. Photo by Keith Geisner

I also had the honor of meeting Eric Jenson and Carl Crank at the 2019 Trailblazer banquet. Photo by Keith Geisner

Always Racing

After the 1978 season, Jim and Stan hung up their helmets. Stan got back to teaching, and Jim became a maintenance supervisor at Flat River Glass Co. It wasn't until 1983 that Jim strapped a helmet back on for competition. On a loaned-out Yamaha IT from none other than Donelson Cycles of Flat River, Missouri, Jim entered the 100-mile Flat River Grand Prix and took fourth overall at the age of forty. A young ISDE racer by the name of Ray Mungenast was also racing that day. Ray won the overall and, within less than a week, would pack up to race the ISDE the following weekend in Wales. Stan Rubottom had partaken in the Grand Prix as well that year but said after the first lap he was done and headed for a dip in the lake.

The Lead Belt News covered the results of the 1983 Flat River Grand Prix. Headlines read: "Grand Prix Major Success."

> More than 300 cyclists competed in the second annual Flat River Grand Prix motorcycle races Saturday and Sunday in St. Joe State Park, a grueling cross-country event that took its toll on men and machine.
>
> A spokesman for the Flat River Chamber of Commerce, sponsor of the event, described the weekend races as another major success. How the organization came out financially was still being figured today, but hopefully the chamber will wind up making money, said Mrs. Vada Coleman. There were many more expenses this year than involved in the promotion of the first race, she explained, but it still looked as though the organization would come out okay.
>
> Local riders came away winning three events, officials said. Don Agnew, of Flat River, took first place in the 250cc class while John McDaniel, of Bonne Terre, won the event for the open class. There was more competition in those two classes than any others, race officials said, based on the number of entries.
>
> Jim Simmons, of Rt. 2, Farmington, who has raced in international competition, finished first in the senior class and 4th overall.
>
> The overall winner, who finished the 100-miles in slightly more than four hours, was Ray Mungenast of St. Louis. He is a son of Dave Mungenast, a major name in motorcycle racing for years. Ray Mungenast will leave for Europe next week to complete in the International Six Day Enduro.
>
> Gayle and Ann Halbrook, who operate Donelson's Cycles in Flat River, were congratulated by chamber officials for their role in organizing the program.

The Halbrooks said from a racing standpoint the weekend was a big success.

Department of Natural Resources also said they felt it was a successful event. The park was closed to other off-road vehicles this weekend for the races. Park Officials said there were no serious problems and both the participants and spectators were well behaved.

The turnout for three-wheelers and mini-bikes for Saturday's races was lower than anticipated, race officials said. Only about 24 three-wheelers entered the competition while 19 mini-bikes entered that race.

Nearly 300 motorcycles showed up for the 100-mile race over the rugged terrain of the state park on Sunday. A new 25-mile course was charted through the park this year, limiting most spectator viewing to the area of Monsanto Lake where two man-made jumps had been constructed for added excitement. The course this year did not go through the area near the Flat River Sports Complex where off-road vehicles are no longer allowed.

Mark Allen of the St. Francois County Ambulance Service said emergency medical technicians provided first aid for a number of riders who suffered minor injuries during the races, but no serious injuries were reported. The ambulance service transported only two victims to an area hospital, one suffering from possible rib injuries and the other from a dislocated finger.

Park rangers and other park personnel were kept busy Sunday trying to locate downed riders and follow up reports of possibly injured cyclists. Their four-wheel drive vehicles were used to take EMTs to those areas that could not be reached by the ambulance.

Park maintenance man Bob McLeod said he was sent looking for a young rider reported down along the power line trail. He found the youth's cycle helmet and race gear, but not the rider. It was after some concern that it was learned the cyclist had found another ride back to the pit area.

Race officials estimated that about half of the 275 riders completed the four laps. The heat and mechanical failures took a heavy toll, they said. It was reported that nearly one-fifth of the cyclists failed to make the first checkpoint after the start of the race, but the dropout rate dwindled after that.

In the competition Saturday, Shawn Skaggs, of St. Louis, won the mini-bike race while Wayne Bradley, of Esther, finished second. The race for three-wheelers was won by Mark Chick, of St. Louis.

Ray Mungenast, of St. Louis, came in the overall winner in Sunday's competition, finishing the course in slightly more than 4 hours.

Other official results announced this morning were:

100cc – Darren Meyers, of the state of Illinois, Lloyd Ridley, of St. Louis and Tracy Burk, of O'Fallon, Ill.

125cc – Chris Burk, of the state of Illinois, Greg Surdyke, of Festus and Matt Jamison, of Granite City, Ill.

xperience steers
yclist to a win

By Jay Crawford
Daily Journal Staff Writer

cing against the clock and the
at the same time can be a
al challenge.

Simmons who won among
r racers in the motorcycle Grand
in St. Joe State Park this month
he was out of shape. At age 40, he
tot been on a motorcycle for five
.

borrowed one after deciding the
ing of the race to try a comeback.
hough Simmons knew his skills
rusty, he also knew he had faced
best riders in the world many
s and won a silver and two bronze
als in the Six-Day Trials in
en, Austria and the United States.
found that experience was riding
him on a day he considered too
or that long of a race, 100 miles.
e track was super-rugged, a type
ad seldom if ever tackled before.
temperature was reported at 96
ees.
t time-tempered skills don't fade
some veterans. "You never
t your rhythm," Simmons said.
e combination of throttle, gas and
es on the turns. It's kind of like
ing. You never forget how to read
errain."

On his way to a four hour, 27 minute,
30 second finish, fourth best among 300
starters, Simmons clung to one
weapon as vital as his skill, concentration. "The minute you start
thinking there's a glass of water 10
miles ahead or what's going to happen
at the finish line, you go down," he
said.

Even with that attitude, he at times
broke his intensity and plunged into
near disaster on the first of four
grueling laps. "Several riders were
stuck on this hill, he recalled. "There
was no reason for it. They should have
shot right up it. I was watching a
couple of them, when whammo." A
tree branch clobbered him over the
eye, leaving a gash that required four
stiches. He ignored blood and again
riveted his mind on riding 100 miles at
top speed.

The branch also knocked the visor
off the cyclist's helmet and ripped off
his goggles.

A breathing space was not to be
found. There was no stretch of the
track to relax on and steel yourself for
the roughest going. All 100 miles were
the roughest going. Looking for a flat,
smooth interval was like expecting a

(See MOTORCYCLE, page 2)

Jim Simmons

Jim's article photo. Photo by The Daily Journal

200cc – Rich Oxten, of Crystal City, Chris Caplinger, of St. Louis and Jimmy Jones, of Union.

250cc – Don Agnew, of Flat River, Dwayne Miinch, of Jackson and Mark Schlett, of Arnold.

Open Class – John McDaniel of Bonne Terre, Ron Kohring, of Illinois and John Hollenberg.

Four-stroke – Tim Arnold, of Ste. Genevieve, Everett Schinault and Wayne Kertz, of Ste. Genevieve.

Seniour Class – Jim Simmons, of Farmington, Gary Surdyke, of Crystal City and Rick Carpentar, of St. Louis. Crawford, J.[21]

• • •

The newspaper clipping Jim found and showed me at our first meeting was from *The Daily Journal*, and it was missing the second page. I was able to reach out to the Missouri State Historical Society and track it down. A month after the 1983 Flat River Grand Prix results were released, a story highlighting Jim's performance, riding ability, and experience was posted. Here is Jim's story from *The Daily Journal*:

Racing against the clock and the years at the same time can be a special challenge.

Jim Simmons who won among the senior racers in the motorcycle Grand Prix in St. Joe State Park this month knew he was out of shape. At age 40, he had not been on a motorcycle for five years.

He borrowed one after deciding the morning of the race to try a comeback.

Although Simmons knew his skills were rusty, he also knew he had faced the best riders in the world many times and won two silvers and a bronze medal in the Six-Day Trials in Sweden, Austria and the United States.

He found that experience was riding with him on a day he considered too hot for that long of a race, 100 miles.

The race was super-rugged, a type he had seldom if ever tackled before. The temperature was reported at 96 degrees.

But time-tempered skills don't fade from some veterans. "You never forget your rhythm," Simmons said. "The combination of throttle, gas and brakes on the turns. It's kind of like dancing. You never forget how to read the terrain."

On his way to a four-hour, 27 minute, 30 second finish, fourth best among 300 starters, Simmons clung to one weapon as vital as his skill, concentration. "The minute you start thinking there's a glass of water 10 miles ahead or what's going to happen at the finish line, you go down," he said.

Even with that attitude, he at times broke his intensity and plunged into near disaster on the first of four grueling laps. "Several riders were stuck on this hill," he recalled. "There was no reason for it. They should have shot right up it. I was watching a couple of them, when whammo." A tree branch clobbered him over the eye, leaving a gash that required four stitches. He ignored blood and again riveted his mind on riding 100 miles at top speed.

The branch also knocked the visor off the cyclist's helmet and ripped off his goggles.

A breathing space was not to be found. There was no stretch of the track to relax on and steel yourself for the roughest going. All 100 miles were the roughest going. Looking for a flat smooth interval was like expecting a hurricane to ease up. "It was the hardest 100-mile scramble I've ever been in," said Simmons, who has competed in the Mojave Desert. "It was either an up or down hill, bumpy or there were rocks or tree roots."

The spot where he cut his head was a 3.5 mile "dozer trail," a swath hacked out of the woods. A tree had evidently fallen across the course during the winter. Branches had been sawed away, but one must have been overlooked.

"St. Joe State Park is an ideal place to have a race of the type offered," Simmons Said. "There are not many 100-mile Grand Prix anywhere. It was a good event."

"Few challengers expected the cruel test of rugged conditions and choking heat," Simmons said. It was reported that 1/5 of the field dropped out before the first check point. Simmons noted that nature gives some people a better cooling system.

Simmons, without any trace of condescension, said many entrants were victims of greenness. "I'm guessing that not over 3 percent had ever ridden 100 miles before," he said.

"Most of them were motocross men, who go as fast for 10 minutes as they can and then rest for 30 minutes. Some were very good motocross racers and very fast, but they had no idea of what they were in for. It becomes not only physical, but mental." Again, showing no disparagement, he classed many of his rivals as "play riders", people who go up to the park on Sunday and have a good time. "They learned something and got their money's worth."

Simmons started out as a "play rider" but advanced to serious efforts, entering several Six-Day Trials, the "Olympics of motorcycle racing." Competitors go 200 miles a day for six days.

Simmons was glad he could rest permanently after St. Joe State Park. He crashed to the ground three times on his third lap, due to lapses of concentration, skinning his shoulder and knee. That plus a black eye and gashed forehead and general fatigue made this his last race.

"I've been through it all," said the senior rider. It's a young man's game. He decided to quit while he's ahead.

Age 40 was the minimum for seniors in the Grand Prix.

He clocked fairly even times for the four circuits. Round two was his slowest as he recuperated from his first loop. "You have to ride a consistent lap," the winner said. "There was probably very little difference in the lap times of everyone in the top 10."

Simmons had no mechanical difficulty with his borrowed 250 Yamaha. There were many flat tires on the track. He refueled for every lap, although he felt he could probably go two on one tank. Dust, although it was thick at times never bothered him seriously.

Leg and hand cramps were severe torment. But again, experience paid off. He knew a cramped leg loses its tightness when extended straight out.

Simmons said his only regular exercise in recent years has been work on his 30-acre "city man's farm" near Esther. He grew up in that area. He is now assistant personnel manager for the Flat River Glass Co., is married and has two children, daughters April and Krista.

Local riders who succeeded in addition to Simmons, included Don Agnew of Flat River and John McDaniel of Bonnet Terre, who won their classes in the Sunday Grand Prix and Wayne Bradley, 15, of Esther, second in Saturday's mini-bike contest.

Simmons is a member of the Central School District Board of Education. He was at the board meeting the day after the race, racing with an agenda.[22]

After the 1983 Flat River Grand Prix, Jim would saddle up one more time during the ISDT reunion ride at St. Joe Park in 2001. Stan would also ride in the same ISDT reunion ride, but this was just the beginning of his second wind.

• • •

In 2008, Stan bought a leftover 2007 Yamaha WR250F. He still lives only a few minutes from St. Joe Park, so what else is a retired ISDT medalist going to do but go riding. It didn't take long before Stan traded in the WR250F for the bigger WR450F, which had the power that could stand up to his competitive riding style. Stan laid out his own challenging six-mile loop within the park. Consistently riding this loop gave him something to gauge his performance against. His competitive nature and the need to succeed has not been lost on him. Today, at the age of seventy-nine, you can still find Stan at St. Joe Park a few days a week riding his loop.

Stan and me after riding at St. Joe Park. Photo by Keith Geisner

In the fall of 2019, I had the pleasure of riding with Stan at St. Joe Park, and even though he says his times are slowing down, it took everything I had to keep up. I was skeptical at first when Stan told me he had a six-mile course he'd been riding since 2008, but after chasing him through the woods and completing three laps, he made me a believer.

Looking at Stan's bike, you can tell he hasn't lost his touch to maintain it since his independent ISDT qualifying days. His bike is spotless. He spares no expense setting it up the way that works for him. He keeps track of his riding hours and has a meticulous maintenance schedule. His bike leaves St. Joe Park as clean as it arrives. I can't say the same thing about his memory of his riding days, but we are still working on that.

Author's Note

While finishing up my Jim Simmons story and getting ready to start the editing process in February 2021, I got an interesting message from someone. Bill Grubin reached out to me with some exciting news that Jim Simmons' 1975 ISDT Rokon had been found. Bill and his friend Mike Johnson from Yakima, Washington, are vintage snowmobile and motorcycle enthusiasts. When Mike discovered the bike at a friend's snowmobile shop, the bike had already been sitting outside since 1994. The current owner bought it for the snowmobile engine parts.

Bill and Mike did their research to find the history on the bike. The bike had the Customer Service Race Bike (CSRB) serial number that only Rokon team riders would have had. The CSRB bikes were built from the ground up for the type of racing they were going to do. The frame also still had the black inspection paint marks with the number 256 scribed into them, which was Simmons' number that year. They were also able to get ahold of Jim Hollander, who confirmed the visual modification done to the bike's frame and the frame color, which was red.

The story behind how the bike made it back to the Unites States is pretty amazing. There was a member of the U.S. military at the 1975 Isle of Man ISDT—his name had been forgotten over the years. The Rokon motorcycle caught his attention because, during the sound test, the officials, not knowing about the Rokon's variable speed transmission, gassed the throttle on one of the team bikes and the bike took off without a rider and into a lake. He was there all week watching the race. At the end of the six-day event, the Rokon team decided to give the bikes away. The U.S. military person grabbed ahold of one as soon as he could. That bike so happened to be Jim Simmons' bike.

The serviceman was able to return the bike to the USA for free on the ship he came home from the service on. The bike spent roughly twenty years in the state of New York, until it was purchased by Mike's friend who runs a snowmobile shop in Minnesota.

The current state of Jim's 1975 ISDT bike is pretty rough, but not bad enough for it to be brought back. The engine and exhaust are missing, but all those items should still be out there. It still has the spoke front wheel on it that Hollander mounted after the front magnesium wheel was damaged during Simmons' accident. Bill and Mike have some decisions to make. Uncovering this historic bike was a miracle in itself, but the steps taken to preserve its history, well, that could fill a book! Will Jim and his 1975 ISDT Rokon ever come together again? I'm sure Jim's head still hurts just thinking about it.

Jim Simmons' 1975 Isle of Man ISDT Rokon discovered. CSRB - 35-1 with race numbers still scribed in the inspection paint dabs. Photo by Mike Johnson

In Closing

In September of 2020, I raced the Lead Belt National Enduro at St. Joe State Park. It marked my twentieth year competing in off-road races. The bike I rode was the 1998 Yamaha WR400F I'd purchased from Surdyke Motorsports twenty years earlier. It was at this race that I was able to meet Ron Ribolzi and Jeff Debell for the first time, and the third rider of the 1978 ISDT Mexico team, Fred Cameron. To be able to meet Fred brought me full circle in this ISDT journey.

Keith Geisner, Fred Cameron, and Jeff Debell after the 2020 Lead Belt National Enduro.
Photo by Keith Geisner

Jim Simmons' #319 Husqvarna will now join Don "Killer" Kudalski's #49 Harley-Davison MX team bike in my collection, and their stories will be preserved along with them. It's interesting how both Jim and Don both have Rokon in common. Jim was one of the first ISDT racers to ride for Rokon, and Don was their first winning motocross racer and went by the nickname "Rokon Don." It's only fitting that while writing Jim's story, I stumbled across a 1973 Rokon RT340, serial number 36, the earliest recorded production serial number on the Rokon registry. We will save serial number 36's story for another time.

In closing, I'm very fortunate to have come across these motorcycles, and I will do my best to make sure their stories will be told for years to come, along with any other special motorcycles that may find me....

Stan Rubottom, Keith Geisner, and Jim Simmons, next to Rokon RT340 serial #36. Photo by Keith Geisner

Endnotes

1 Francis, R. (2018.) THE INTERNATIONAL SIX DAYS TRIAL (THE I.S.D.T.) THE OLYMPICS OF MOTORCYCLING. Accessed 12/20/2020.
https://thetenterdenanddistrictmuseum.wordpress.com/2018/01/14/the-international-six-days-trial-the-i-s-d-t-the-olympics-of-motorcycling/.

2 Youngblood, E. (2006.) Take It to the Limit: The Dave Mungenast Way. St. Louis, MO: Motohistory.

3 Youngblood, E. (2000.) John Penton and the Off-Road Motorcycle Revolution. North Conway, NH: Whitehorse Press.

4 Gallagher, B. (1999.) "The True History of Rokon Motorcycles." Accessed 5/5/2021.
http://rokonworld.com/history.html.

5 American Motorcyclist Association.
www.motorcyclemuseum.org.

6 Magazine Staff. "Hall of Famer: Leroy Winters." AMERICAN MOTORCYCLIST. October 2018. Accessed 5/52021.
https://magazine.americanmotorcyclist.com/5874/hall-of-famer-leroy-winters/.

7 Newspaper Staff. "Simmons Wins National Cycle Endurance Event." The Daily Journal. September 16, 1971. Pg. 2.

8 Reynolds, B. "The AMA and the USA Pass the Test." Cycle News. October 31, 1972. Pg.14.

9 Morey, C. "The American Team Warranty: Six Days or 1200 Miles, Whichever Comes First!" Cycle News. September 21, 1976. Pg. 20.

10 Mann, S. "The almost Six Days Trial." American Motorcyclist. December 1978. Pg.40.

11 DiPrete, M. "Rokon Record?" Cycle News. October 8, 1974. Pg. 4.

12 Newspaper Staff. "Simmons And Clark Take Gold." The Daily Journal. April 13, 1973. Pg. 3.

13 Newspaper Staff. "Local Riders to Attempt Qualify for International Team." The Daily Journal. July 6, 1973. Pg. 4.

14 Slover, R. "ISDT Beckons Local Riders." The Daily Journal. June 12, 1975. Pg. 5.

15 Weems, J. "Simmons, Rubottom Again Make U.S. Team for Six-Day Trials." The Daily Journal. September 1, 1976. Pg. 8.

16 Morey, C. "Six Days a Week." Cycle News. October 12, 1976. Pg. 17.

17 Morey, C. "Six Days a Week" Cycle News. October 12, 1976. Pg. 17.

18 Wealey, P. "The Latest Poop." Cycle News. March 1, 1978. Pg. 2.

19 Holeman, D. "The Magic Wrench behind Yamaha's ISDT Project." Cycle Magazine. March 1977. Pg. 54.

20 Holeman, D. "The ISDT IT400, Six Weeks in Solitary Yielded Six Days of Success." Cycle Magazine. March 1977. Pg.49.

21 "Grand Prix Major Success." The Daily Journal. September 18, 1983. Pg. 1.

22 Crawford, J. "Experience Steers Cyclist to a Win." The Daily Journal. October 3, 1983. Pg. 1.

DISCOVERING SIX DAYS

KEITH GEISNER

Printed in the USA
CPSIA information can be obtained
at www.ICGtesting.com
LVHW071952011224
798067LV00009B/317